# 2 BUSINESS VENTURE

## WORKBOOK

**Roger Barnard & Jeff Cady**

Nina Leeke

OXFORD
UNIVERSITY PRESS

T0352837

# OXFORD
UNIVERSITY PRESS

Great Clarendon Street, Oxford OX2 6DP

Oxford University Press is a department of the University of Oxford.
It furthers the University's objective of excellence in research, scholarship,
and education by publishing worldwide in

Oxford  New York

Auckland  Cape Town  Dar es Salaam  Hong Kong  Karachi
Kuala Lumpur  Madrid  Melbourne  Mexico City  Nairobi
New Delhi  Shanghai  Taipei  Toronto

With offices in

Argentina  Austria  Brazil  Chile  Czech Republic  France  Greece
Guatemala  Hungary  Italy  Japan  Poland  Portugal  Singapore
South Korea  Switzerland  Thailand  Turkey  Ukraine  Vietnam

OXFORD and OXFORD ENGLISH are registered trade marks of
Oxford University Press in the UK and in certain other countries

© Oxford University Press 2009

The moral rights of the author have been asserted

Database right Oxford University Press (maker)

First published 2009
2018
10 9 8

**No unauthorized photocopying**

All rights reserved. No part of this publication may be reproduced,
stored in a retrieval system, or transmitted, in any form or by any means,
without the prior permission in writing of Oxford University Press,
or as expressly permitted by law, or under terms agreed with the appropriate
reprographics rights organization. Enquiries concerning reproduction outside
the scope of the above should be sent to the ELT Rights Department, Oxford
University Press, at the address above

You must not circulate this book in any other binding or cover
and you must impose this same condition on any acquirer

Any websites referred to in this publication are in the public domain and
their addresses are provided by Oxford University Press for information only.
Oxford University Press disclaims any responsibility for the content

ISBN: 978 0 19 457810 3

Printed in China

ACKNOWLEDGEMENTS

*The authors and publisher are grateful to those who have given permission to reproduce
the following extracts of copyright material*: p 41 information about Vegawatt.
Copyright © 2009 Owl Power Company. All Rights Reserved. Reproduced by
kind permission; p 21 information about Koc Holding A. S. from www.koc.
com.tr. Reproduced by kind permission; p 29 extract from *Pushing the Envelope*
by Pamela Rohland, March 1999, from *Entrepreneur Magazine*. Reproduced by
permission of Entrepreneur Media Inc; p 53 extract from *Season's Meetings*
by Letitia Baldrige, originally published in *Success Magazine*, December 1998.
Reproduced by kind permission of Letitia Baldrige.

*Sources*: p 22 statistics from www.oica.net; p 6 information from www.
bridgestone.co.jp, www.tommy.com, www.ibm.com

*Cover image courtesy of*: Alamy/Image Source.

*We would also like to thank the following for permission to reproduce the following
photographs*: Alamy Images pp 6 (Ferrari F1 car/Claude Thibault), 6 (Tommy
Hilfiger logo/David Anthony), 7 (Business people outdoors/Stock Connection
Distribution), 19 (Image Source Black), 24 (Car keys/Mladen Curakovic), 24
(Travel alarm clock/Darby Sawchuk), 24 (Coffee maker/Alison Thompson) 39
(TongRo Image Stock), 50 (David R. Frazier Photolibrary, Inc.);Webb Chappell
© 2009 p 29 (Carla Ventresca); Corbis pp 6 (IBM's research laboratory/
Alessandro Della Bella/Keystone), 45 (Everett Kennedy Brown/Epa), 60
(Randy Faris), 63 (Corporate training/C. Willhelm/Photex/zefa); Getty pp
4 (James Hardy/PhotoAlto Agency), 9 (Image Source), 14 (Bruce Laurance),
29 (Tony Metaxas/Asia Images), 34 (Image Source), 55 (Image Source); OUP
pp 37 (Hotel maid/Tim Pannell/Corbis), 43 (Sao Paulo, Brazil/Photodisc), 57
(Business meeting/Photodisc); Owl Power Company p 41; Photolibrary pp 50
(Colleagues holding a blueprint/Image Source), 52 (School canteen/Jacques
Loic/Photononstop); PunchStock p 62 (Businessman speaking at podium/Blend
Images); Rex Features p 24 (AA/SB/Keystone USA); Sony p 25.

*Illustrations by*: Javier Joaquin/The Organisation pp 4, 36.

*We would also like to thank the folowing for their valuable contribution*: Jeffrey C.
Fryckman and Dorothy E. Zemach.

# Contents

**1**   Meeting people     4

**2**   Telephoning     9

**3**   Schedules and appointments     14

**4**   Company performance     19

**5**   Products and services     24

**6**   Talking about decisions     29

**7**   Complaints and problems     34

**8**   Checking progress     39

**9**   Future prospects     45

**10**   Regulations and advice     50

**11**   Meetings and discussions     55

**12**   Speaking in public     60

     Answer key     65

# Meeting people

## MODULE 1.1

**1** Match the pictures (1–4) to the questions (a–h). There are two questions for each picture.

a   Are you enjoying the party? ☐

b   Do you fly a lot? ☐

c   Do you stay here often? ☐

d   Did you go to any presentations this morning? ☐

e   Are you going to Canada on business? ☐

f   Is your room OK? ☐

g   What's on the program tomorrow? ☐

h   Can I get you another drink? ☐

**2** Match the questions in Exercise 1 to the answers below.

☐ 1 Yes, I do. It's central and the rates are very reasonable.
☐ 2 No, I'm visiting my brother in Vancouver.
a 3 Yes, thanks, I'm having a great time.
☐ 4 There's a talk on e-commerce in the afternoon.
☐ 5 Yes, mostly to the States.
☐ 6 Yes, just one. It was about market research.
☐ 7 Thanks. A glass of white wine, please.
☐ 8 Yes, it's very comfortable, thank you.

## MODULE 1.2 · Introductions

Put the words in the sentences in the correct order.
a don't / hello / met / we've / I / think .
b know / do / other / each / you ?
c Jim Murray / is / the / this / from / office / Boston .
d long / you / been / waiting / have ?

## MODULE 1.3 · Developing a conversation

**1** Complete the conversation between two people at a reception in Tokyo. Use the words below.

from   to   on   for   by   of   with   in

**A** *How long are you staying in Japan?*
**B** *I'm here _____¹ a week. Do you live in Tokyo, Mr. Ueda?*
**A** *No, I live in Saitama. It's just north _____² Tokyo. Where are you _____³ in the United States?*
**B** *I live _____⁴ Detroit. I'm here _____⁵ business. I'm _____⁶ IBM.*
**A** *Oh really? And are you going to spend all your time in Tokyo?*
**B** *No, I'm going _____⁷ Nagoya _____⁸ bullet train on Sunday.*

**2** You are in San Francisco on a business trip. Answer your host's questions. Give as much information in your answers as you can.
a Did you have a good flight?

_____

b What do you think of San Francisco?

_____

c Is your hotel OK?

_____

d Would you like something to drink before we start the meeting?

_____

e We have some free time on Friday. Is there anything you'd like to do?

_____

Read these descriptions of three companies and complete the questions below.

**International Business Machines (IBM)** started up in 1924. It is the world's top provider of computer hardware. The company makes a broad range of computers, including PCs, notebooks, mainframes, and network servers. It is also the world's second largest software producer. Over 60% of its revenue comes from outside the US.

**Bridgestone** is a Japanese company. It is one of the world's largest tire and rubber manufacturers, and supplies tires to Ford and General Motors. Bridgestone is a leading tire maker for large trucks, heavy equipment, and aircraft. 20% of its sales come from non-tire products, including sporting goods and materials for earthquake-proof buildings.

In 1989 New York designer Tommy Hilfiger and Hong Kong-based manufacturer Silas Chou became partners, and formed the **Tommy Hilfiger Corporation**. The company sells not only men's and women's casual and sportswear, but also fragrances, belts, and bedding. It is now expanding into the home furnishing and cosmetics markets.

a When _____?
   In 1924.

b What _____?
   Personal computers, notebooks, mainframes, and network servers.

c Does _____?
   Yes, it does, and also General Motors.

d How much _____?
   20 percent.

e Where _____?
   In Hong Kong.

f Which markets _____?
   Home furnishing and cosmetics.

## MODULE 1.5 — Finishing a conversation

Put the sentences into the right order to make two conversations.

**1**
  a  Well, it was nice meeting you. ☐
  b  Sure. I'll do that. ☐
  c  That would be nice. Give me a call next time you're in town. ☐
  d  Yes, we should meet again sometime. ☐

**2**
  a  No problem. Go ahead. ☐
  b  Thank you. I'm very sorry, but I have to make a phone call. Would you excuse me? ☐
  c  … And here's our new brochure. ☐

## MODULE 1.6 — At a reception

Two people are meeting for the first time. Complete the questions in their conversation.

**A**  *Hello, I don't think we've met. I'm Shen Young.*

**B**  *Nice to meet you. I'm Laura Waite from Toronto. Are you _____ _____¹ conference?*

**A**  *Yes, there are some interesting presentations. Is this your _____ _____ _____² Korea?*

**B**  *No, I came here last year as well. Who do _____ _____³ for?*

**A**  *A company called CleanCare. And _____⁴?*

**B**  *I work for NP Papers. We make paper hygiene products. What does your _____⁵ do?*

**A**  *We sell hygiene solutions.*

**B**  *Interesting. Well, it was nice talking to you. Hope to see you again.*

**A**  *Nice meeting you too. Bye.*

**1** Put the sentences in the correct order to make an introductory e-mail.

a I will be in Perth next week and would like to meet you to discuss possibilities for working together. ☐

b Dear Ms Addison, ☐

c I hope you have time to meet me. Please let me know when would be good for you. ☐

d We produce a variety of plastic products for household use. We have two factories in Australia. We plan to introduce our products in Western Australia in the near future. ☐

e Best regards, ☐

f Sylvia Jones. ☐

g I'm the Business Development Manager at 'PP Plastics'. You may remember that we met at the 'Plastics for the Future' fair recently. ☐

**2** Write an e-mail introducing your company to a new partner.

**3** Abbreviations of the words on the left are commonly used in written correspondence. Circle the correct abbreviation for each item.

1 in care of    a c/o    b c-o    c c.o.

2 company    a Comp.    b Co.    c Cy.

3 corporation    a Cor.    b Corp.    c Co.

4 department    a dep.    b dpt.    c dept.

5 incorporated    a Inco.    b Incorp.    c Inc.

6 limited    a Lim.    b Ltd.    c Ld.

7 number    a No.    b Nu.    c Num.

**4** The abbreviations below are often used in less formal correspondence. Match them with the correct answers.

a acct.        1 administration

b admin.       2 continued

c conf.        3 meeting

d cont.        4 manager

e intl.         5 attention

f mfg.        6 account

g mgr.        7 international

h mkt.        8 week

i mtg.        9 enclosure

j wk.         10 manufacturing

k attn.       11 conference

l enc.        12 market

# 2

# Telephoning

**MODULE 2.1**  ## Calling contacts

Read this telephone conversation. Choose the more polite way of saying the same thing. Check (✔) the correct answers.

**A** *I want to speak to Ann Jones.*  ☐
*Hello. Could I speak to Ann Jones, please?*  ☐

**B** *I'm afraid she's away from her desk right now.*  ☐
*She isn't here. I don't know where she is.*  ☐

**A** *So when will she be there?*  ☐
*I see. Do you know when she'll be back?*  ☐

**B** *I don't know.*  ☐
*I'm sorry, I don't know.*  ☐

**A** *Could I leave a message?*  ☐
*I want to leave a message.*  ☐

**B** *Well, I guess that's OK. What's your name?*  ☐
*Of course. May I have your name, please?*  ☐

**A** *Vic Kaplan. Ask her to call me today.*  ☐
*Vic Kaplan. That's K-A-P-L-A-N. Could you ask her to call me today?*  ☐

**B** *I'll give her your message, Mr. Kaplan.*  ✔
*Sure.*  ☐

**A** *Thank you very much. Goodbye.*  ☐
*OK.*  ☐

## MODULE 2.2

### Making a call

Underline the correct forms in the two extracts from telephone conversations.

**A** *Hello, **Max Pitt speaking / I'm Max Pitt**[1].*

**B** *Hello, this is Kaito Kimura from MM Motors.*

**A** *Hello, Mr Kimura. **What can I help / What can I do for you**[2]?*

**B** *I speak about / I'm calling about[3] our order.*

**A** *Good afternoon, MM Motors.*

**B** *Good afternoon. **Could I speak to / Would I speak to**[4] Max Pitt, please?*

**A** ***Moment / One moment**[5], please.*

**A** *I'm afraid he's **not in his desk / not in the office**[6] right now.*

**B** *Could you **put me through to / connect me**[7] his assistant, please?*

**A** *Sure. No problem.*

## MODULE 2.3

### Leaving a message

Tom Asher's assistant took some messages for him. Read the messages and complete what the caller said.

Examples

**Caller** *"This is John Dodd. Could you ask Tom to call me this afternoon?"*

**Message** *Mr. Dodd called. Please call him this afternoon.*

**Caller** *"My name is Miki Obata. Could you tell Tom that the machine parts will arrive next week?"*

**Message** *Ms. Obata called. The machine parts will arrive next week.*

a  "_____?"

Mr. van Donk called. Please send him the new catalogue as soon as possible.

b  "_____"

Mr. Chung called. His new e-mail address is ddchung@asek.com.

c  "_____"

Rosa Velasquez called. She'll return the damaged items on Monday.

d  "_____?"

Mr. Shibata called. Please fax him his flight details.

e  "_____?"

Mr. Neff called. Please meet him at Harry's Bar at 8:00 p.m.

**MODULE 2.4**     Voicemail messages

Read the voicemails for Tom Asher and write messages for him.

Example

> ## V⊙ICEMAIL
>
> *"Hello, Tom. This is Charlene Brown. Could you call me back as soon as possible, please? I need to talk to you before Tuesday's meeting."*
>
> **Message**
>
> *Charlene Brown called. Please call her asap.*
> *She needs to talk to you before Tuesday's meeting.*

a   "Hi Tom. It's Bobby Deng. Sorry, but I'm running late. I won't get to the reception until about 8p.m."

Message _____

b   "Hello. This is Meryl Woo from Woo Enterprises. I'm sorry, but our computer system has crashed. Could you send me your order by fax, please? Thank you."

Message _____

c   "Hi Tom. It's Tony here. Have you got Sharon White's phone number? If so, could you send it to me asap, please? Thanks."

Message _____

d   "Hello. This is a message for Tom Asher. Mike Kibby from the Hotel Plaza speaking. I'm calling about your conference booking for next week. I need a few more details. Could you call me back, please? It's 234-5788. Thank you."

Message _____

**MODULE 2.5**     Taking a message

Choose the correct form to complete the questions.

Could I     Could you     Would you like to

a   _____ speak to Mr Shibata, please?
b   _____ have your name, please?
c   _____ hold?
d   _____ put me through to her assistant, please?
e   _____ leave a message?
f   _____ have your number, please?
g   _____ spell your company name, please?

# MODULE 2.6

## Where's John?

Find the four mistakes in the message below which John's assistant left for him, after the following telephone conversation.

| | |
|---|---|
| **Assistant** | *Hello, Wallace Enterprises.* |
| **Jill** | *Hello, this is Jill Murray from M-Trade Thirty Three. Could I speak to John Wallace, please?* |
| **Assistant** | *Sorry, he's out of the office now. Can I take a message?* |
| **Jill** | *Yes, please ask him to call me. I'll be in the office until seven o'clock.* |
| **Assistant** | *OK, what's your phone number?* |
| **Jill** | *Double nine three four seven six eight. Extension two five eight.* |
| **Assistant** | *I'll give him the message. Thanks, bye.* |
| **Jill** | *Thank you, goodbye.* |

*Jill Murray from M-Trade 43 called. Please call her back before 6p.m. Her number is 883-4768, extension 248.*

# MODULE 2.7

## Business writing: telephone messages

**1** Tom Asher found this message on his desk when he returned to the office. Read the message and answer the questions. Write short answers.

---

### WHILE YOU WERE OUT

| | |
|---|---|
| **Message for** Tom Asher | Taken by Polly Yang |
| Time 11:30a.m. | Date March 21 |
| **Message from** Mr. Takagi | Company Toshiba |
| Tel. No. | Ext. |
| ✓ will call back later | ☐ please call him / her |

**Message**
It's about his visit next week. It's not urgent.

---

a  Who is the message for? _____

b  Who took the message? _____

c  What time did she write it? _____

d  Who called? _____

e  Which company does he work for? _____

f  Will he call again? _____

g  What did he call about? _____

h  Is it urgent? _____

**2** Now complete the message form below. Use this voicemail:

'Message received: 3:55 p.m, April 27. Hello, this is Tina Spinner from MV Music. This is a message for Sam Cash. Please call me back urgently on 912-1985. I need to talk to you about the new contract. Thank you.'

## WHILE YOU WERE OUT...

**Message for** _____

Taken by _____

Time _____  Date _____

**Message from** _____

Company _____

Tel. No. _____  Ext. _____

◯ **will call back later**          ◯ **please call him / her**

**Message**

**3** A client calls your co-worker while he / she is out of the office. Complete the message form for the call. Use your own ideas.

## WHILE YOU WERE OUT...

**Message for** _____

Taken by _____

Time _____  Date _____

**Message from** _____

Company _____

Tel. No. _____  Ext. _____

◯ **will call back later**          ◯ **please call him / her**

**Message**

# 3

# Schedules and appointments

**MODULE 3.1**   Talking about schedules

1   Adam Ho works in the publicity department of a large insurance company.
Today is Monday, April 2nd. This morning Adam had a meeting with a
designer, Shirley Hasan. Read the notes he made during the meeting.

> **Schedule for new catalogue**
>
> APRIL
>
> Tuesday 3                  finalize the copy
> Wednesday 4                check the artwork
> Thursday 5                 meeting with the printers
> Friday 6                   photo shoot (all day with Shirley)
> Saturday 7/Sunday 8   select the photos
> Thursday 12 (latest!)  send the catalogue copy to the printers
> Tuesday 17                 get the catalogue proofs from the printers

2   Shirley lost her notes and telephoned Adam on Tuesday to check the
schedule. Complete the sentences using the information from Adam's notes.

| | |
|---|---|
| **Shirley** | *I just wanted to check the schedule for the catalogue. We're doing the photo shoot the day after tomorrow, right?* |
| **Adam** | *Well, no, Shirley,* <u>I'm doing the photo shoot this Friday.</u>                    1 |
| **Shirley** | *And you're choosing the photos sometime next week.* |
| **Adam** | *Actually, _____*    2 |
| **Shirley** | *Oh, yes, of course. And you're meeting the printers today.* |
| **Adam** | *Actually, _____*    3 |
| **Shirley** | *But you're sending the catalogue copy to the printers by next Friday, right?* |
| **Adam** | *Actually, _____*    4 |
| **Shirley** | *Ah, yes, now I remember. And the printers are sending the proofs to you next month.* |
| **Adam** | *Actually, _____*    5 |

**1** On Tuesday 3rd Adam sent his boss, Diane Stone, an e-mail message. Complete the message using the words below. Use the information above to help you.

next Thursday      the day after tomorrow      tomorrow      this weekend
today      a week from next Tuesday      this Friday

---

✉ **E-mail message**

**Date:**      Tuesday April 3, 2009, 09:05
**From:**      Adam Ho
**To:**        Diane Stone
**Subject:**   Schedule for the new catalogue

Diane,

I had a meeting with Shirley Hasan yesterday about the new catalogue. I'm finalizing the copy _____¹. I'm checking the artwork _____². The meeting with the printers is _____³. We're doing the photo shoot _____⁴, so I can select the best ones _____⁵. I hope to send everything to the printers by _____⁶, so the proofs should be ready _____⁷.

Adam

---

**2** Now write four sentences about yourself using the time phrases below. Use real or imaginary information.

Example
on Friday
_I'm visiting a client on Friday._

the day after tomorrow

_____

this weekend

_____

next Monday

_____

a week from next Wednesday

_____

## MODULE 3.3

Today is Monday 21st. Complete Yusuf's conversation with Paul using his diary below.

**Diary**

| Monday 21 | Tuesday 22 | Wednesday 23 | Thursday 24 | Friday 25 |
|---|---|---|---|---|
| TODAY | Team building training | Conference | Work at home | Dentist |
| **Monday 28** | **Tuesday 29** | **Wednesday 30** | **Thursday 31** | **Friday 1** |
| training | 9am Management meeting<br><br>2pm Sales presentation | Work at home | | |

| | |
|---|---|
| **Paul** | *How about meeting tomorrow?* |
| **Yusuf** | *Sorry, I'm attending a training course.* |
| **Paul** | *OK. What about the day after tomorrow?* |
| **Yusuf** | *Sorry, _____.* [1] |
| **Paul** | *And how about next Wednesday?* |
| **Yusuf** | *I'm afraid I'm busy. _____.* [2] |
| **Paul** | *OK. And next Tuesday?* |
| **Yusuf** | *Sorry, _____.* [3] |
| **Paul** | *And in the afternoon?* |
| **Yusuf** | *I'm afraid _____.* [4] |
| **Paul** | *OK. Are you free next Thursday?* |
| **Yusuf** | *Yes, that's fine. How about 9:30?* |
| **Paul** | *Great. See you then.* |

## MODULE 3.4

Put the sentences in the correct order to make a conversation. The first sentence is numbered for you.

**B** *OK, Monday afternoon?* ☐

**A** *So, when can we have the team meeting?* ☐ 1

**A** *Sorry, after lunch we're making a presentation. It's a really tight schedule.* ☐

**A** *Well, the visitors are leaving on Wednesday. How about Thursday at 10 o'clock?* ☐

**B** *Great. See you then.* ☐

**A** *Sorry, we're meeting the visitors from head office on Monday morning.* ☐

**B** *How about at the beginning of next week, Monday?* ☐

**B** *I see. How about at the end of the week then?* ☐

**MODULE 3.5**

Antonio and Ruby need to reschedule their meeting. Write their telephone conversation.

Antonio: answers the phone.
*Hello. Antonio speaking.*

Ruby: greets Antonio. Gives her name.

Antonio: greets Ruby.

Ruby: explains she can't go to the meeting on 27th. Gives reason.

Antonio: says he understands.

Ruby: suggests a new day and time.

Antonio: says the time is not good for him. Gives a reason. Suggests another day or time.

Ruby: agrees. Confirms.

Antonio: says he looks forward to meeting. Says goodbye.

Ruby: says thank you and goodbye.

**MODULE 3.6**

Finding a free day

Choose the word which doesn't go with the verb.

Example

| 1 | arrange | a meeting / ~~a telephone~~ / a time |
| 2 | attend | a trade fair / a meeting / a visit |
| 3 | have | lunch / a time / another appointment |
| 4 | go | sailing / on a tour / tennis |
| 5 | play | swimming / golf / football |
| 6 | give | a presentation / a speech / a meeting |

**1** Read the e-mail messages and answer the questions below. Write short answers.

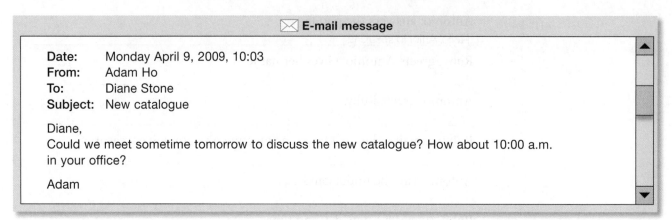

✉ **E-mail message**

**Date:**     Monday April 9, 2009, 10:03
**From:**    Adam Ho
**To:**       Diane Stone
**Subject:**   New catalogue

Diane,
Could we meet sometime tomorrow to discuss the new catalogue? How about 10:00 a.m. in your office?

Adam

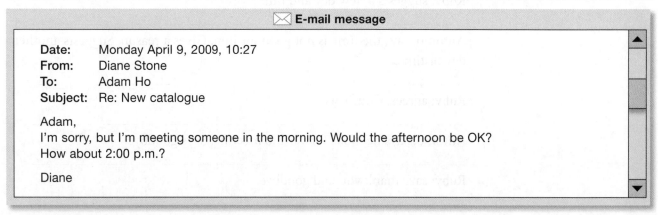

✉ **E-mail message**

**Date:**     Monday April 9, 2009, 10:27
**From:**    Diane Stone
**To:**       Adam Ho
**Subject:**   Re: New catalogue

Adam,
I'm sorry, but I'm meeting someone in the morning. Would the afternoon be OK? How about 2:00 p.m.?

Diane

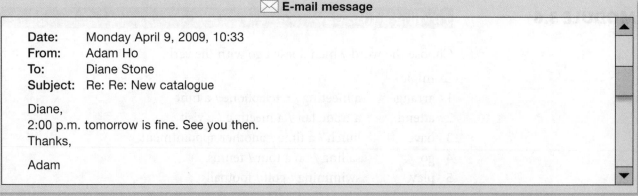

✉ **E-mail message**

**Date:**     Monday April 9, 2009, 10:33
**From:**    Adam Ho
**To:**       Diane Stone
**Subject:**   Re: Re: New catalogue

Diane,
2:00 p.m. tomorrow is fine. See you then.
Thanks,

Adam

a   Who is the first message from?     _____

b   What does he want to talk about?   _____

c   When does he want to meet?     _____

d   Why can't she meet him then?    _____

e   When can she meet him?      _____

f   Can Adam meet her then?      _____

**2** Now write three similar e-mail messages to make an appointment with a colleague. Use real or imaginary information. The first message is from you.

# Company performance

**MODULE 4.1** Presenting figures

Match the presentation slides (1–4) and the sentences (a–d).

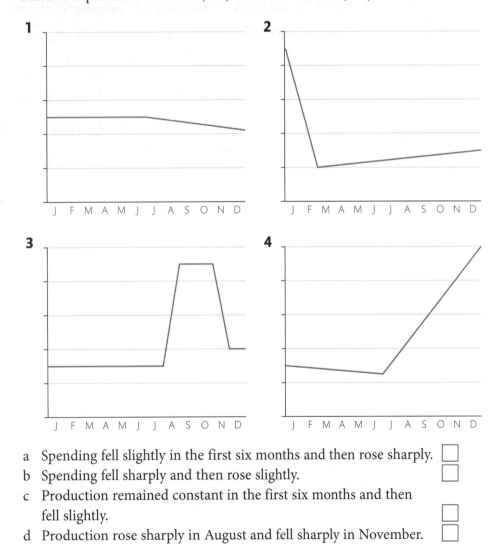

a Spending fell slightly in the first six months and then rose sharply. ☐
b Spending fell sharply and then rose slightly. ☐
c Production remained constant in the first six months and then
   fell slightly. ☐
d Production rose sharply in August and fell sharply in November. ☐

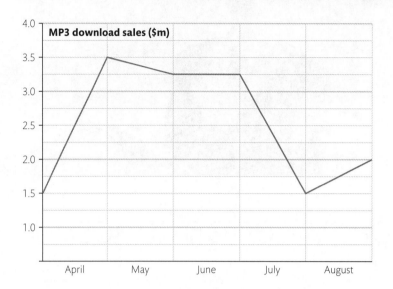

**1** Look at the graph and complete the report on MP3 download sales at discountMP3s.com. Use the words below.

rose slightly     rose sharply     remained constant     fell slightly     fell sharply

MP3 download sales were very uneven last year. In April sales _____¹ from $1.5 million to $3.5 million. In May they _____² to just over $3 million. In June sales _____³ but _____⁴ in July to just under $1.5 million. In August they _____⁵ to $2 million.

**2** Now use the graph below to write a short report on footwear sales. Use the report in Exercise 1 to help you.

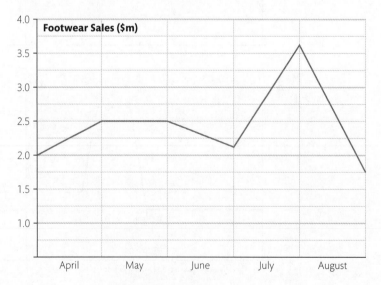

Read the two texts about the Turkish company Koç (pronounced *coach*). The first text is correct. The second text has five mistakes in it. Look at the second text and check (✓) the numbers which are correct, then rewrite the numbers with mistakes in them correctly.

The Koç Group is Turkey's largest industrial conglomerate, in terms of revenue, profits, and exports. It is Turkey's largest employer, with **90,000**[1] employees. It is also the **49th**[2] largest company in Europe. In **2007**[3] **5**[4] of the top **10**[5] companies in Turkey were part of the Koç group, according to the annual survey by the Istanbul Chamber of Commerce.

In **2007**[6] the revenues of the group increased by **5%**[7] to **$39.5 billion**[8]. Net profits grew by **275%**[9]. The group's exports account for **11%**[10] of all of Turkey's exports.

As part of its corporate social responsibility, the group supports vocational high schools, providing scholarships for **4,000**[11] students in **250**[12] high schools.

---

The Koç Group is Turkey's largest industrial conglomerate, in terms of revenue, profits, and exports. It is Turkey's largest employer, with **eighty thousand**[1] employees. It is also the **forty-ninth**[2] largest company in Europe. In **two thousand and seven**[3] **five**[4] of the top **ten**[5] companies in Turkey were part of the Koç group, according to the annual survey by the Istanbul Chamber of Commerce.

In **one thousand and seven**[6] the revenues of the group increased by **five percent**[7] to **twenty-six point five billion**[8] dollars. Net profits grew by **two hundred and fifty-five**[9] percent. The group's exports account for **eleven percent**[10] of all of Turkey's exports.

As part of its corporate social responsibility, the group supports vocational high schools, providing scholarships for **one million**[11] students in **two hundred and ninety**[12] high schools.

1  [X]  ninety thousand          7  [ ]  _____
2  [✓]  _____          8  [ ]  _____
3  [ ]  _____          9  [ ]  _____
4  [ ]  _____          10 [ ]  _____
5  [ ]  _____          11 [ ]  _____
6  [ ]  _____          12 [ ]  _____

## MODULE 4.4 — Comparing information

**World motor vehicle production (in thousands)**

|       | 2002  | 2003  | 2004  | 2005  | 2006  |
|-------|-------|-------|-------|-------|-------|
| USA   | 5,019 | 4,510 | 4,230 | 4,321 | 4,366 |
| UK    | 1,630 | 1,658 | 1,647 | 1,596 | 1,442 |
| Japan | 8,618 | 8,478 | 8,720 | 9,017 | 9,757 |

**1** Are these sentences true or false? Check (✓) the correct answers.

|   |   | True | False |
|---|---|------|-------|
| a | The USA produced more cars in 2004 than in 2005. | ☐ | ☐ |
| b | Japan produced more cars in 2002 than in 2003. | ☐ | ☐ |
| c | Japan produced fewer cars than the USA in 2005. | ☐ | ☐ |
| d | The UK's best year was 2003. | ☐ | ☐ |
| e | The USA's production was highest in 2003. | ☐ | ☐ |
| f | Japan's production was lowest in 2003. | ☐ | ☐ |

**2** Write three true sentences comparing the motor vehicle production figures in Exercise 1.

a _____

b _____

c _____

## MODULE 4.5 — Presenting information

Look at the graph and complete the sentences using the words below.

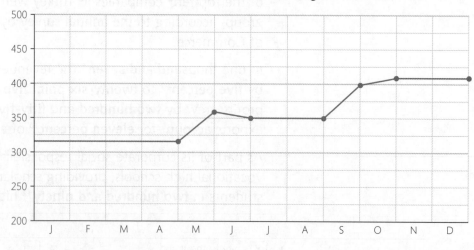

by (2)    to (5)    at    from

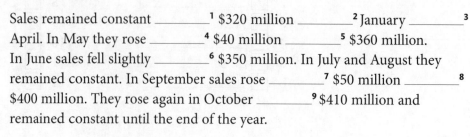

Sales remained constant _____¹ $320 million _____² January _____³ April. In May they rose _____⁴ $40 million _____⁵ $360 million. In June sales fell slightly _____⁶ $350 million. In July and August they remained constant. In September sales rose _____⁷ $50 million _____⁸ $400 million. They rose again in October _____⁹ $410 million and remained constant until the end of the year.

**UNIT 4** Company performance

**1** Read the e-mail message and answer the questions below. Write short answers.

---

✉ **E-mail message**

**From:**    Kay Ashton
**To:**      Pierre Levin
**Subject:** Our meeting

Dear Pierre,

I'd like to apologize for canceling our meeting on Wednesday on such short notice. I hope it didn't inconvenience you too much. My car broke down on the expressway, and I had to wait an hour for a tow truck.

How about meeting early next week, say Monday at 10:00 a.m.?
I look forward to hearing from you, and apologies once again.

Kay

---

a  Who is apologizing?        _____

b  Why?                       _____

c  What is her excuse?        _____

d  Does she suggest another time?  _____

**2** Write a similar message apologizing to a business acquaintance. Use the information below.

You are writing to Tanya Jacobs. You canceled a meeting last Friday on short notice because you had to attend an emergency meeting. You suggest a meeting on Thursday at 2:00 p.m.

---

✉ **E-mail message**

**From:**    ............................................
**To:**      ............................................
**Subject:** ............................................

............................................................

............................................................

............................................................

............................................................

............................................................

............................................................

---

# Products and services

**MODULE 5.1**  Product features

**1** Match the sentences (a–i) to the correct products (1–3). There are three sentences for each product.

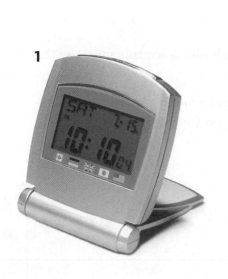

a  It's designed for car owners. ☐
b  It's designed for the home office. ☐
c  It's designed for international travelers. ☐
d  One special feature is the permanent filter. ☐
e  It can display 24 global time zones. ☐
f  It protects your car from thieves. ☐
g  It has a handy snooze feature. ☐
h  You can lock your car remotely. ☐
i  It comes with a colorful ceramic mug. ☐

Read this description of a product and complete the questions below.

## SONY'S VPL-CS21 PROJECTOR

This product is essential for people who need to make presentations when they're on business trips. The VPL-CS21 Projector allows you to project an image from a laptop computer onto a large screen. It's only 5.2 cm high and fits easily inside a briefcase. It weighs a little under 2kg. It has different picture modes, for home and business use and its 3LCD technology provides natural colour, bright images, and clear detail.

The projector has an Intelligent Auto Setup function, which saves your personal settings and allows you to start presenting straight away. You'll spend less time worrying about your equipment, so you have more time to focus on your presentation. It costs about $900.

a  What _____?
   It can project computer images across a room.

b  How _____?
   It's quite small. It can fit inside a briefcase.

c  Who _____?
   It's designed for business people who need to make presentations when they're on business trips.

d  Where _____?
   You can use it at home or at work.

e  Does _____?
   Yes, a special feature is the automatic set up function.

f  How _____?
   It costs about $900.

## MODULE 5.3

### Talking about company activities

Write descriptions of the two companies based on the notes below.

Example

**Company:** Motorola

Business type: telecommunications

Company HQ: Schaumburg, Illinois, USA

Employees: approximately 66,000

Activities: range of telecommunications and entertainment products
    and services

Motorola is a telecommunications company. The headquarters are in Illinois, USA and they have approximately 66,000 employees. They offer a range of telecommunications and entertainment products and services.

**Company 1:** Hyundai

Business type: automobile

Company HQ: Seoul, Korea

Employees: more than 137,000

Activities: car production and research

**Company 2:** Marriott International

Business type: hotel industry

Company HQ: Washington D.C. USA

Employees: approximately 151,000

Activities: more than 3000 hotels
    and resorts worldwide

## MODULE 5.4

### Talking about services

1 Complete the conversation. Use the words below.

use    developing    design    successful    install    provide    help

**A** *Can you tell me something about your business?*

**B** *Well, in general we _____[1] a range of Internet services to companies.*

**A** *For example?*

**B** *We _____[2] websites and act as a consultant for companies who want to _____[3] the Internet in their business.*

**A** *What does that involve?*

**B** *We _____[4] companies to plan their online services and we also_____[5] hardware and software.*

**A** *Is your consulting business _____[6] ?*

**B** *Yes, it's the fastest-growing part of our company.*

**A** *And what are your plans for the future?*

**B** *We're _____[7] our own Internet sales software. It's coming out next month.*

2 Write a short description of a service company you know or an imaginary company.

_____

_____

**MODULE 5.5**

**1** A manager and training company representative are having a meeting about organizing English lessons at the manager's company. Match the first and second parts of the phrases to make questions.

| | | |
|---|---|---|
| a | Can I | lessons do they want a week? |
| b | Would you like | the lessons be in our office? |
| c | What | get you something? |
| d | Where | will it cost? |
| e | How | a coffee? |
| f | How many | are your plans for next year? |
| g | How much | will the office be? |
| h | Will | old are they? |

**2** Match the answers below to the questions above.

☐ 1 We're going to open a new office in Canada.

☐ 2 Most of them are in their 30s.

[a] 3 Just some water, thanks.

☐ 4 I'm not sure exactly. I'll send you a price.

☐ 5 Yes, a coffee would be great thanks.

☐ 6 Three a week, I think.

☐ 7 Yes, if it's easier for you.

☐ 8 In Vancouver.

**MODULE 5.6**

**1** A customer wants to buy something, but can't remember the name of the product, so he describes it to the sales assistant. What is the product?

*It's quite small – a little bigger than a cell phone. It's made of metal and plastic. I think it's quite expensive. You can use it in the car. Taxi drivers usually have one. It tells you where to go.*

**2** You want to buy a microwave oven , but can't remember the word. Write a description of it.

_____

_____

**3** Unscramble the letters to make the names of some everyday products.

r / o / t / i / i / d / y / n / a / c     _____

s / u / t / t / h / o / b / o / r / h     _____

p / t / l / o / a / p     _____

y / e / c / i / c / b / l     _____

**1**   Match the parts of the letter (a–j) to the headings (1–10).

a
APEX
OFFICE PRODUCTS
1625 SE Park Ave
Philadelphia, PA 18125

b   Ref. 100/75 XC
c   November 15, 2009

d   Ms. Gloria Duveen
Purchasing Manager
GEP Inc.
1215 Winchester Drive
Baltimore, MD 22101

e   Dear Ms. Duveen,

f   Thank you for taking the time to speak with me on the telephone yesterday.

As promised, I have enclosed our new catalogue and price list. Please do not hesitate to contact me if I can be of any further assistance.

I look forward to hearing from you.

g   Sincerely,

h   *Erica Deng*

i   Erica Deng
Marketing Assistant

j   Enc.

1   date line          —        6   signature          —
2   body of the letter  —        7   salutation         —
3   enclosure line      —        8   letterhead         —
4   complimentary close —        9   inside address     —
5   reference number    —        10  signature block    —

**2**   Now match the descriptions below with the correct headings in Exercise 1.

a   This tells you if there are any other pieces of paper in the envelope.  _3_

b   This is a polite way of finishing the letter.  —

c   This is the address of the person who receives the letter.  —

d   This tells you when the letter was written.  —

e   This tells you the name and address of the company the writer works for.  —

f   You should include this information when you reply to a letter.  —

g   You usually find the writer's position in the company here.  —

# 6

# Talking about decisions

## MODULE 6.1      An industry history

**1**   Read the text and circle the correct answers.

**Carla Ventresca** was a young copywriter with an advertising agency in Boston. *Because / So*¹ she didn't earn a lot of money, she started making her own greetings cards. Her friends liked her cards very much *because / and*² they asked her to make cards for them.

In 1993 she took samples of her work to a local card shop, and as a *result / because*³ the owner agreed to put them on her shelves. *Because / And*⁴ the cards sold well, she started up her own company, Carla Cards, the same year. After a few years sales decreased *so / because*⁵ she consulted friends about her designs. As a *result / And*⁶ she created some completely new designs which featured a range of humorous characters. The new cards were very popular, *and / because*⁷ business improved. She now sells her cards to stores in the USA and Canada.

**2** Now answer the questions about Carla's business.

a Why did she start making her own greetings cards?

Because *she didn't earn a lot of money.*

b Why did her friends ask her to make greeting cards for them?

Because _____

c Why did she set up Carla Cards in 1993?

Because _____

d Why did she consult her friends about her designs?

Because _____

e Why did business improve?

Because _____

## MODULE 6.2

## Cause and effect

Use the words below to connect the phrases and make sentences about the Kiwiwire company.

and    as a result    so    because

Examples
demand increased    moved to a bigger factory
*Demand increased so Kiwiwire moved to a bigger factory.*
*Kiwiwire moved to a bigger factory because demand increased.*

| | |
|---|---|
| sales rose | profits increased sharply |
| demand increased | carried out an advertising campaign |
| profits rose sharply | employees received a bonus |
| had problems with quality control | demand fell |

1 _____

2 _____

3 _____

4 _____

5 _____

6 _____

7 _____

8 _____

Complete the crossword.

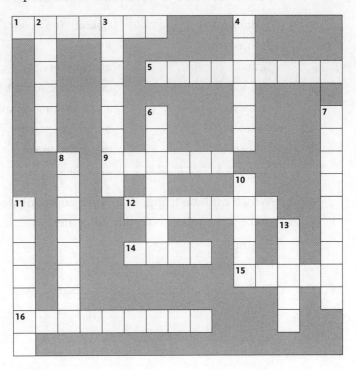

**Across**

1   The company earned record _____ last year. Investors were very happy.

5   We managed to reach _____ after a long meeting.

9   We plan to _____ our business by opening 20 new branches next year.

12  The company had problems with quality _____ and sales fell.

14  Sales of the D500 model were good last year but demand _____ this year.

15  Our market _____ is around 15%.

16  In our company we always try to achieve a _____ before we decide to do something important.

**Down**

2   We modernized operations, and as a _____, production increased.

3   In my department everyone is _____ in making decisions.

4   We used to meet once a month but now we have _____ meetings, every Thursday.

6   To _____ means to get better.

7   Sales _____ sharply last year. In fact, they rose by 60%.

8   Last month we had a big advertising _____ on TV and radio.

10  All the employees in my company got a _____ of $500 this year.

11  To _____ more customers we reduced our prices.

13  Nike, Sony, and Levi's are all world-famous _____ names.

## MODULE 6.4 | Explaining decisions

**1** Match the verbs in Column A to the nouns in Column B.

| Column A | Column B |
|----------|----------|
| protect | a book |
| attract | a luxury service |
| launch | business customers |
| publish | an advertising campaign |
| offer | brand recognition |
| improve | the environment |
| carry out | a product |

**2** Which of these things does your company do? Use the words in the box to make sentences about your company.

Example

My company carries out advertising campaigns.

1 _____

2 _____

3 _____

4 _____

5 _____

## MODULE 6.5 | Franchises

**1** Two partners are talking about starting a business. Choose the correct forms to complete their conversation.

**A** *Shall we buy / Shall we buying*¹ *a Dream Ice Cream franchise?*

**B** *No, I'm not think so / I don't think so*². *There are already some ice cream stores in this area. How about buying / How about to buy*³ *a BB's Burgers franchise?*

**A** *No, people doesn't need / people don't need*⁴ *so much unhealthy food. I'm interesting for / interested in*⁵ *healthy food. What about buying a Green Bean Bar?*

**B** *No, there are too many cafes and restaurants in the town. What do you think to buy / of buying*⁶ *a Family Fitness Club? There aren't any sports clubs in the area.*

**A** *That's a good idea. I think it would be very successful / success*⁷.

**2** What kind of business would you open in your town and why?

_____

_____

_____

**1** Read this letter and answer the questions below. Use short answers.

**≡JCE Supplies**
888 Springfield Road
San Francisco, CA 95104

October 10, 2009

Neumann Electronics
Mecklenburgische Str. 53
14197 Berlin
Germany

Dear Mr. Neumann,

I am writing to inform you that we have not received your payment of $2,468.75 for invoice no. B238 which, according to our records, I mailed to you on August 3rd. I hope that you received the invoice.

For your convenience, I have enclosed another copy with this letter. I look forward to receiving the payment from you by the end of the month. If there are any problems, please do not hesitate to contact me.

Sincerely,

Luigi Pavesi

Luigi Pavesi
Accounts Dept.

Enc.

a When did Mr. Pavesi's company mail the invoice? _____

b How much does Mr. Neumann's company have to pay? _____

c Has Mr. Pavesi sent another invoice with the letter? _____

d When does Mr. Pavesi ask for payment to be made? _____

**2** Now write a similar reminder letter. Use the information below and your own name.

| | |
|---|---|
| Client company: | Compusol |
| Address: | P.O. Box 155, Birmingham BS1 7AF, UK |
| Contact: | David Corney |
| Invoice number: | N2860 |
| Amount: | $5,468.50 |
| Payment due: | December 5 |
| Previous contact: | E-mail, September 26 |
| Date today: | October 15 |

# Complaints and problems

**MODULE 7.1**

## Receiving a complaint

Read the sentences below. Who says them? Write (C) for customer and (S) for supplier.

1  I'm very sorry about that. —
2  I'm afraid I have a complaint about … —
3  What seems to be the problem? —
4  Could you give me a few details? —
5  We ordered the Q200 model, but you sent the Q500. —
6  I understand there's a problem with last week's delivery. —

**MODULE 7.2**

## Making a complaint

1  Put the lines of the telephone conversation in the correct order.

**A** *How can I help you, Mr. Akman?* ☐

**B** *I'd appreciate that. Thank you. Goodbye.* ☐

**A** *I'm sorry to hear that. What's the problem?* ☐

**A** *Good morning, Conex Customer Service.* ☐ 1

**A** *Goodbye.* ☐

**B** *Yes. When we make double-sided copies, it jams every time.* ☐

**B** *Good morning. This is Mesut Akman from Alpha Engineering.* ☐

**A** *The paper jams?* ☐

**A** *I see. I'm very sorry about the inconvenience. I'll send someone round right away.* ☐

**B** *The paper jams.* ☐

**B** *I'm afraid I have a complaint about the new photocopier you installed yesterday.* ☐

**2**   Complete the e-mail. Use the words below.

wrong   inconvenience   unfortunately   complaint
problem   appreciate   damaged   care

Last month we made a _____[1] about a delivery of computer keyboards.
Some of the keyboards were _____[2], so I called the shipping department
and told them about the _____[3]. They apologized for the _____[4] and
promised to take _____[5] of everything right away. The replacements
arrived the following day, but _____[6], they sent the _____[7] amount! If
you can tell me the name of a good supplier, I'd _____[8] it!

# MODULE 7.3

## Dealing with a complaint

**1**   Complete the conversation. Use the information in the order form.

| Customer | Order number | Date | Amount | Item | Model number |
|---|---|---|---|---|---|
| Takeda Golf | 043762 | Sept. 28 | 25̶ 35 | Golf bag | DB306 |

**A**   *Good afternoon, Sportworld Wholesales. How can I help you?*

**B**   *Good afternoon, This is Akira Sato from Takeda Golf here. I'm afraid there's a problem with our last order.*

**A**   *I'm sorry to hear that. Could you give me the order number?*

**B**   *Yes, it's _____[1].*

**A**   *One moment, please. Yes, according to our records, you placed the order on _____[2]. You ordered 25 _____[3], model number _____[4].*

**B**   *I'm afraid that's not quite correct. We ordered _____[5] golf bags, not _____[6].*

**A**   *I'm sorry about that. I'll look into it right away.*

**B**   *Thank you.*

**2**   Now use this order form to write a similar conversation.

| Customer | Order number | Date | Amount | Item | Model number |
|---|---|---|---|---|---|
| Uno Sports | 044812 | Oct. 4 | 300 | baseball | B̶X̶3̶0̶3̶ BX403 |

**A**   *Good afternoon, Sportworld Wholesales. How can I help you?*

**B**   _____

**A**   *I'm sorry to hear that.* _____

**B**   _____

**A**   *One moment, please.* _____

_____

_____

**B**   _____

_____

**A**   _____

**B**   _____

**1**  Match the complaints (a–f) to the responses (g–l) and the pictures (1–6).

**Complaints**

a  Excuse me, but this is dirty.

b  But you said it would be ready today.

c  I bought this here yesterday, but some pages are missing.

d  I'm afraid these aren't my photos.

e  I've just arrived from Paris, and one of my bags is missing.

f  I tried to watch this DVD last night, but it didn't work.

**Solutions**

g  I'm sorry. We made a mistake with the names.

h  Oh, I'm very sorry. Please fill in this lost baggage form and we'll try to help you as soon as we can.

i  Hm, I'll check if it has a scratch.

j  Oh, I'm sorry. I'll get you a clean one right away.

k  I'm really sorry. It'll be ready tomorrow, and we'll give you a discount.

l  Oh, I'm sorry about that. I'll get you another copy.

**2**  Now write two complaints and solutions using the pictures below.

1  **A** _____

   **B** _____

2  **A** _____

   **B** _____

**MODULE 7.5**

Hotel problems

**1** Put the words in the correct box to make problems in a hotel.

cold   towels   lamp   hot water   noisy   mini-bar   Internet   coffee

| There isn't any ... | There aren't any ... | The ... isn't working. | The room is ... | The ... is empty. |
|---|---|---|---|---|
|  |  |  |  |  |

**2** Put the words in the correct order to make complaints and solutions.

1   A   any / there / pillows / aren't .

    B   room / send / I'll / right away / your / some / to .

2   A   working / isn't / air con / the .

    B   someone / I'll / right / send / away .

**MODULE 7.6**

Business writing: a letter of complaint

**1** Complete the sentences. Use the words below.

apologize   clearly   suggest   polite   possible

When you write a complaint letter, fax, or e-mail, you should ...

• send the complaint as soon as _____¹.

• explain the situation _____².

• _____³ a way of solving the problem.

• do not _____⁴ for complaining.

• be _____⁵.

**2**   Read the e-mail.

---

✉ **E-mail message**

**Date:**      February 28, 2009
**To:**         Daphne Choi
**From:**      Pablo Bazo
**Subject:**   Order number E276

Dear Ms. Choi,

I am writing with reference to the delivery of digital cameras, order number E276, which we received this morning.

Unfortunately, you sent us the wrong amount. We ordered 30 K60 digital cameras, but we received 20. I am attaching a copy of the order form for your reference.

I would be grateful if you would send ten more cameras as soon as possible.

I hope that future orders will be checked carefully before dispatch.

Sincerely,
Pablo Bazo

---

**3**   Answer the questions. Use short answers.

a   Which order is Pablo Bazo writing about?

_____

b   When did his company receive the cameras?

_____

c   What is the problem?

_____

d   What is Mr. Bazo attaching with the e-mail?

_____

e   What does Mr. Bazo want Ms. Choi to do?

_____

**4**   Now write a similar e-mail to George O'Hara. Use this information and your own name:

computer monitors – order no. BN56 – received yesterday
sent the wrong model – we ordered the PS25 monitor – received the PS20 –
please send us the correct model as soon as possible

# 8

# Checking progress

**MODULE 8.1** | Travel arrangements

Look at Dan's checklist for Cindy's trip to India.

> ## checklist
> reserve flights ✓
> make hotel reservations ✓
> arrange meeting with Mr Mehra ✗
> reserve table for dinner ✓
> get a gift ✓

Now complete the conversation by putting the verbs into the correct form.

**A** *How are you doing with my travel arrangements for the trip to India?*

**B** *Fine. I _____¹ (reserve) all your flights.*

**A** *Thanks. And what about hotels?*

**B** *Yeah. I _____² (made) reservations at the Taj in Mumbai and the Intercontinental in Delhi.*

**A** *Sounds good. And the meeting with Mr Mehra?*

**B** *I _____³ (arrange) an appointment with him yet. He's busy at the moment, but I'm going to speak to him soon.*

**A** *OK. And what about the dinner on the first night?*

**B** *Don't worry. I _____⁴ (book) a table for four at the Taj.*

**A** *That's great. One more thing – should I take a gift for Mr Mehra?*

**B** *I know – don't worry. I _____⁵ (buy) something nice for him.*

**A** *Perfect. Thanks for your help.*

**MODULE 8.2**  Getting an update

**1** Your company is going to open a new hotel soon. Complete your questions to the project manager using the words below.

Have you     How's     How are

1 _____ the project going?
2 _____ the builders doing?
3 _____ finished the restaurant yet?
4 _____ the manager getting on?
5 _____ thought about the gym yet?
6 _____ started the garden yet?

**2** Match the questions (1–6) to the answers (a–f).
☐ a  Fine. He's started recruiting staff.
☐ b  Not yet. We're going to work on the garden last.
☐ c  Pretty good. Everything's on schedule.
☐ d  Almost. We're going to finish it next month.
☐ e  Fine. They've finished the major work.
☐ f  Yes. We've already ordered some sports equipment.

**MODULE 8.3**  Giving an update

Your boss is on a business trip and sends you the e-mail below. Use your notes to write your reply.

✉ **E-mail message**

Dear _____

The trip is going well. How are you doing in the office? Have you finished preparing next week's presentation? How about the conference trip? Have you booked my tickets and hotel? And, please don't forget to book a taxi from the airport.

Thanks. See you soon.

Kim

presentation ✓
flight tickets ✓
hotel ✗ – tomorrow
taxi ✗ – tomorrow

**1**  Read the article about a new business.

> new business

## GREEN KITCHEN

> Vegawatt is a new product which recycles dirty cooking oil and produces energy at the same time! It is the idea of James Peret, who previously worked as a Product Development Engineer. James spent four years developing Vegawatt in his garage, and is CEO of Owl Power Company which sells the product.

The first Vegawatt has been sold to a seafood restaurant in Massachusetts, where they are very happy with it. The owner says "The Vegawatt system enables me to significantly reduce my energy costs, generate clean energy on-site, and very importantly, reduce the heavy energy footprint of my restaurant."

The Vegawatt unit takes used oil, filters it, and combusts it to make electricity. The electricity can provide power for kitchen equipment and hot water. The unit is about the same size as a refrigerator and costs about €22,000. It may seem expensive, but it can reduce a restaurant's electricity bill by 20%. In addition, the restaurant saves money by not having to pay for used oil collection.

Out of the
deep fryer
into your pocket!

Your waste oil is the key to utility cost savings!

**2**  Are the following statements true (T) or false (F)?

a  Vegawatt uses dirty cooking oil to produce electricity.  ☐

b  James Peret works as a product development engineer.  ☐

c  James developed Vegawatt over fourteen years.  ☐

d  The restaurant owner is happy with Vegawatt because
it saves the restaurant money and produces energy.  ☐

e  Vegawatt can reduce the energy bill of a restaurant by about 20%.  ☐

**1** Look at the project schedule for a new restaurant and mark the sentences true (T) or false (F). Correct the false answers.

Example

They are going to design the menu in March.

[F] *They designed the menu in January.*

## Project schedule

| | January | February  NOW | March | April |
|---|---|---|---|---|
| design the menu | ✓ | | | |
| decorate the rooms | | | ✓ | |
| recruit staff | | ✓ | | |
| start advertising | ✓ | | | |
| install equipment | | | | ✓ |

1 They installed equipment in January.

☐ _____

2 They are going to decorate the rooms in March.

☐ _____

3 They are going to recruit staff in April.

☐ _____

4 They are going to start advertising in March.

☐ _____

**2** Think of a project in your company and answer the questions below.

1 What have you already done?

_____

2 What are you doing now?

_____

3 What are you going to do?

_____

**MODULE 8.6**

Cindy Bennett has just arrived in São Paulo. She calls her assistant, Dan Rubin, at headquarters. Circle the correct answers.

**A**  *Hello, Dan? How are things?*

**B**  *Everything's fine, Cindy. Are you at the hotel?*

**A**  *Yes, I just **checked / check**[1] in.*

**B**  ***Have you had / Did you have**[2] a good flight?*

**A**  *It was OK, but the food **hasn't been / wasn't**[3] great.*

**B**  *That's too bad. **Did / Have you heard**[4] from Mr. Viana yet?*

**A**  *Yes, there **was / has been**[5] a message at reception when I **have arrived / arrived**[6]. He wants to reschedule the meeting. I **called / I'm calling**[7] him a number of times but there's no reply.*

**B**  *Have you **seen / saw**[8] the e-mail from Ms. Park?*

**A**  *No, I **didn't / haven't**[9] checked my e-mail yet. Why?*

**B**  *She **phoned / has phoned**[10] before lunch.*

**A**  *Did she **left / leave**[11] a message?*

**B**  *No, she **said / has said**[12] she would e-mail you.*

**A**  *OK, thanks, Dan. Please e-mail or phone me if there are any problems.*

**B**  *Sure, Cindy.*

**MODULE 8.7**

**1**  When we write an itinerary, we usually write notes, using important words only. We often leave out punctuation and articles (*a*, *an*, *the*).

Examples

You will meet Sherry Tong in the Far Eastern Hotel lobby.

• meet Sherry Tong in Far Eastern Hotel lobby

You will have lunch in the factory cafeteria.

• lunch in factory cafeteria

**2**  Now read the e-mail and the itinerary.

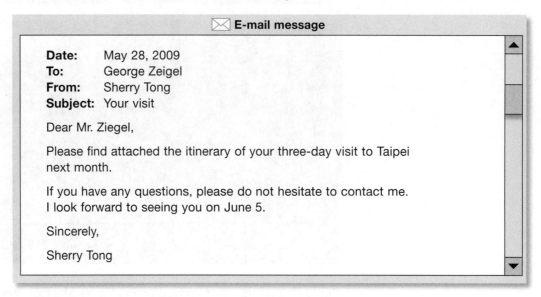

**E-mail message**

**Date:**  May 28, 2009
**To:**  George Zeigel
**From:**  Sherry Tong
**Subject:**  Your visit

Dear Mr. Ziegel,

Please find attached the itinerary of your three-day visit to Taipei next month.

If you have any questions, please do not hesitate to contact me. I look forward to seeing you on June 5.

Sincerely,

Sherry Tong

George Ziegel: Itinerary, June 5–7          (approx. = approximately)

**Monday, June 5     TAIPEI**

| | |
|---|---|
| 8:00 | meet Sherry Tong in Far Eastern Hotel lobby<br>taxi to TEC factory, Taipei |
| 9:30–11:30 | factory tour |
| 12:00 | lunch in factory cafeteria |
| 13:00–14:30 | presentation |
| 15:00–18:00 (approx.) | planning meeting |
| 18:00 | taxi to hotel |
| 19:30 | meet Michael Chen in lobby |
| 20:00 | dinner with Mr. Li at Orchid restaurant |

**3**  Complete the sentences using the information in the itinerary.
  a  Mr. Ziegel is staying at the _____ Hotel.
  b  He is going to the TEC factory by _____ .
  c  The factory tour will take _____ hours.
  d  His presentation begins at _____ .
  e  The planning meeting is scheduled to last about _____ hours.
  f  Michael Chen will meet him in the lobby at _____ .
  g  He's going to have dinner with _____ .

**4**  Write an itinerary for a one-day visit by a foreign guest to your company or school.

# Future prospects

**MODULE 9.1**

### Forecasting

Complete these sentences about your country next year.

Example

the price of food will rise / fall

*Next year in (Japan) I think the price of food will rise.*

1  companies will take on more / fewer workers

_____

2  the price of gas will go up / down

_____

3  inflation will rise / fall

_____

4  the stock market will be stable / unstable

_____

5  unemployment will rise / fall

_____

6  the currency become stronger / weaker

_____

**Predicting trends**

**1** Put the words in the right order to make sentences.
In thirty years' time …

1 want / think / electric cars / will / I / people

_____

2 you / newspapers / do / people / think / will / read ?

_____

3 work / people / at home / will / most

_____

4 don't / smoke / people / think / I / will

_____

5 demand / don't / there / I / fixed line telephones / for / think / any / will be

_____

**2** What do you think? Write your opinion on each sentence.
Example
1   _I think people will want electric cars, because they are green._
2   _____
3   _____
4   _____
5   _____

**MODULE 9.3**

**Instant decisions**

Write replies to each sentence using one of the verbs below.

watch    go    phone    ~~look at~~    help    send    pay

Example

1  A  Here's your travel itinerary.
   B  _Thanks, I'll look at it later._

2  A  I don't understand the homework.
   B  _____

3  A  There's a good movie on TV tonight.
   B  _____

4  A  We need to change the time of the next English lesson.
   B  _____

5  A  Have you finished that report? I really need it as soon as possible.
   B  _____

6  A  I heard that the station is closed.
   B  _____

# MODULE 9.4     Financial advice

**1** Put the letters in the correct order to make words. All the words are used to show how certain we are about the future.

1 ileendyfti   _definitely_      5 barpyblo   _____

2 yam   _____      6 githm   _____

3 etranci   _____      7 resu   _____

4 docvennic   _____      8 killey   _____

**2** Now use the words above to complete the sentences. There may be more than one correct answer.

a I'm _____ that profits will fall next year.

b It's _____ that the economy will get stronger.

c In my opinion, the president will _____ resign soon.

d The London branch _____ close by the end of the year.

e Prices _____ won't increase much next year.

# MODULE 9.5     Long-term future

**1** Complete the table about your future.

| Do you think you will ... | Definitely | Probably | Maybe | Probably Not | Definitely Not | When? |
|---|---|---|---|---|---|---|
| move to a different city? | | | | | | |
| have your own business? | | | | | | |
| be famous? | | | | | | |
| start a new hobby? | | | | | | |
| work abroad? | | | | | | |
| work for a different company? | | | | | | |
| buy a new car? | | | | | | |
| make a million dollars? | | | | | | |
| learn another language? | | | | | | |

**2** Write sentences using the information from the table.

Example

1 <u>I think I'll probably move to another city sometime.</u>

2 _____

3 _____

4 _____

5 _____

6 _____

7 _____

8 _____

9 _____

## MODULE 9.6

### Wall Street

**1** Complete the notes about the two companies using the words below.

in (x2)    for    of (x2)    at    on

a **Sunshine Stores:**
 a chain ___ supermarkets
 known for good products ___ a reasonable price
 are spending a lot ___ expansion – buying supermarkets internationally
 Share price: €10 / share

b **Lux Autos:**
 specialize ___ making luxury cars
 good reputation ___ quality
 cost ___ skilled workers is high
 are investing a lot ___ research (cars of the future)
 Share price: €20 / share

**2** You have €10,000 to invest. Which company will you buy shares in and why?

_____

_____

**1** Read this letter from a musical instrument manufacturer to a music store manager.

---

✉ **E-mail message**

October 23, 2009

Hobbs Music Center
125–7 Broome St
Perth 6162

Dear Mr. Hobbs,

It was a pleasure to meet you the other day. As you requested, I am sending you our new catalogue.

I would like to draw your attention to our new electronic keyboards on page 45. We think the Nashville model, with its range of 50 exciting rhythms will be very popular this year.

If you have any questions or would like to inspect any of our new products, please do not hesitate to contact me.

Sincerely,

Kay Scott

Kay Scott
Sales and Marketing Department

---

**2** Are the following sentences true (T) or false (F)?

a  Kay Scott met Mr Hobbs a long time ago. ☐

b  Mr Hobbs asked Kay Scott to send him a catalogue. ☐

c  Kay Scott thinks Mr Hobbs is interested in electronic keyboards. ☐

d  The Nashville keyboard has been very popular this year. ☐

e  Mr Hobbs is going to contact Kay Scott soon. ☐

**3** You are a sales representative with a cosmetics company. Write a similar letter to a drugstore manager. Use the information below and your own name.

Ms. Henderson – meet / last week – next year's catalogue
New lipsticks on page 3 – Serena line – wide range of brand new colors – be a top seller next year.

# Regulations and advice

## MODULE 10.1 — Job requirements

**1** Read this interview with an architect.

**A** Could you tell us about how to become an architect in the USA?

**B** I'd be glad to.

**A** First of all, what kind of knowledge and skills does an architect need?

**B** The ideal architect should be good at science, mathematics, and design, and also have a broad knowledge of the world. Of course, this is not always the case, and some architects have only average math skills, for example.

**A** I guess you have to be able to draw well?

**B** Well, it's an important skill, but you can easily learn it.

**A** How about foreign languages?

**B** Most architecture schools don't require them, but speaking at least one foreign language will obviously help if you want to study or work abroad.

**A** The training is pretty long, isn't it?

**B** Yes. You have to be very motivated, because it may take as long as ten years to qualify as an architect. And you have to work very hard – there isn't much time for working part-time or having fun! You have to study at least five years in school, and then work as a paid intern.

**A** That's a kind of trainee?

**B** Right. You work for an architectural or related office, and receive a salary.

**A** And how long does the internship last?

**B** Three years.

**A** Can you work as a qualified architect after that?

**B** Well, you have to take an examination first. If you pass, then you can work as a qualified architect.

**2** Are these statements true or false?

|  |  | True | False |
|---|---|:---:|:---:|
| a | You can become an architect if you have average ability in math. | ☐ | ☐ |
| b | It's difficult to learn to draw. | ☐ | ☐ |
| c | An architect doesn't have to speak a foreign language. | ☐ | ☐ |
| d | An architecture student has to be motivated. | ☐ | ☐ |
| e | To become an architect, you have to study for at least ten years. | ☐ | ☐ |
| f | Most architecture students can't do part-time jobs. | ☐ | ☐ |
| g | You have to work at least five years as an intern. | ☐ | ☐ |
| h | You can work as a qualified architect immediately after you graduate from architecture school. | ☐ | ☐ |

# MODULE 10.2    Traveling by plane

**1** Read the information about getting to and from London Heathrow Airport.

○ **London Underground**
It takes approximately 55 minutes to get to central London from the airport on the Piccadilly line. The last train leaves Terminals 1, 2, 3 at 11:48 p.m. (11.30 p.m. on Sundays)

○ **Heathrow Express**
Trains link Heathrow with Paddington Station in central London, and run every 15 minutes. Tickets can be bought on the Internet, at the station, or on the train itself.

○ **Heathrow Connect**
This train service links Heathrow with local train stations in West London. Fares start at £4.90 (adult single). You must buy your ticket before boarding as a penalty fare zone operates between Hayes & Harlington and London Paddington.

○ **Hotel Hoppa**
This bus service collects passengers from outside each terminal and takes them directly to many hotels in central London. The fare is £4 for adults and 50 pence for children.

○ **Taxis**
There is a black cab taxi rank outside each terminal. An average fare to central London costs between £45 and £70, and the journey takes about one hour.

**2** Now complete the sentences. Use the words below.

can   can't   have to   don't have to

a   There are underground, bus, and train services from Heathrow Airport, and you _____ also take a taxi.

b   You _____ use the underground after midnight.

c   You _____ wait more than 15 minutes for the Heathrow Express train.

d   You _____ book your ticket on the Heathrow Express online.

e   If you are using Heathrow Connect, you _____ buy your ticket before you get on the train.

f   If you use the Hotel Hoppa from Heathrow, you _____ worry about transportation when you arrive in central London.

g   If you want to go to central London by taxi, you _____ pay at least £45.

## MODULE 10.3

### Company regulations

Use the words below to complete the sentences about your workplace.

can   can't   have to   don't have to

In my company employees …

1   _____ wear a uniform.

2   _____ go on business trips.

3   _____ work on Saturdays.

4   _____ choose when to take their vacation.

5   _____ learn English.

6   _____ have a university degree.

7   _____ work overtime.

8   _____ eat in a staff canteen.

9   _____ smoke in the office.

**MODULE 10.4**

Read the advice about going on a long flight. Which sentences are not good advice? Re-write them to give good advice.

1 It's a good idea to drink alcohol during the flight.

_____

2 Try to move around a lot during the flight.

_____

3 It's better if you eat a lot during the flight.

_____

4 It's best not to wear comfortable clothes.

_____

5 You should drink a lot of water during the flight.

_____

6 You shouldn't get to the airport in plenty of time.

_____

7 Try not to adjust to the new time zone as soon as possible.

_____

8 I'd eat a lot of fatty foods before the flight.

_____

**MODULE 10.5**

Giving advice

**1** Read this extract from an article in an American business magazine.

*To be a good party guest, you should...*

**Answer the invitation as soon as you can.**
➡ Reply within a week.

**Arrive on time.**
➡ Arrive no more than ten minutes late.

**Leave on time.**
➡ Leave at 7 p.m. If the party ends at 7 p.m.

**Drink only a little alcohol.**
➡ Drink no more than one beer or mixed drink per hour.

**Talk to people.**
➡ Go up to people you don't know and introduce yourself.

**Apologize if you accept and don't attend.**
➡ Contact the host the next day.

**2** Write a question and answer for each piece of advice.

a    <u>Do you think I should answer the invitation as soon as I can?</u>
     <u>Oh, yes. It's a good idea to reply within a week.</u>

b    _____
     _____

c    _____
     _____

d    _____
     _____

e    _____
     _____

f    _____
     _____

## MODULE 10.6    Business writing: cultural advice

You receive the following e-mail from an overseas colleague. Write a reply.

---

✉ **E-mail message**

Dear _____

I'm writing to ask for your advice.

I'm really looking forward to my visit to your country as I've never been there before.

Could you give me some tips for my visit, please? Firstly, what should I bring?

Secondly, I'd like to know something about the work culture, for example, attitudes to time, what I should wear in the office.

Finally, is there anything I should know if I'm invited to a party or to someone's home?

Thanks so much for your help.

Looking forward to seeing you.

Shane

---

✉ **E-mail message**

Dear Shane

....................................................................................

....................................................................................

....................................................................................

....................................................................................

Best regards

---

# Meetings and discussions

**MODULE 11.1**

## Suggestions

**1** Match the topics (a–h) to the correct suggestions (1–8).

a   Business travel costs
b   Future prospects
c   Company restaurant
d   Hiring procedures
e   Quality control
f   Real estate costs
g   Production costs
h   After-sales service

1   I think we should run stricter checks.
2   Maybe we should advertise vacancies on our web page.
3   I think we should use frequent flyer programs as much as possible.
4   How about appointing more authorized agents?
5   Why don't we invest more in R&D?
6   How about hiring a nutritionist for advice?
7   Why don't we share our office space with another company?
8   Maybe we should manufacture more parts in-house.

**2** Write down five suggestions to improve your company.

1   _____
2   _____
3   _____
4   _____
5   _____

**1**   Complete the dialogues from a sales meeting at a computer store. Use the words below.

about    suggestions    think    agree    idea    should

1   **A** I think we should change the store layout.

    **B** I don't _____ I agree.

2   **A** How _____ including more free software?

    **B** I don't think we should do that.

3   **A** Why don't we increase advertising?

    **B** That's a good _____.

4   **A** Does anyone have any _____?

    **B** Well, why don't we offer a free set-up service?

5   **A** Maybe we _____ offer more options.

    **B** I'm not sure about that.

6   **A** I think we should try to increase Internet sales.

    **B** I _____.

**2**   Complete the sentences about the dialogues in Exercise 1. In some sentences there is more than one possible answer.

a   In dialogue(s) _____, speaker A asks for some ideas.

b   In dialogue(s) _____, speaker B agrees with A's idea.

c   In dialogue(s) _____, speaker B makes a suggestion.

d   In dialogue(s) _____, speaker B doesn't agree with A's idea.

**3**   Match the expressions on the left to the expressions on the right that have the same or similar meaning.

a   I think we should ...                          1   I'm sorry, but I can't agree with that.

b   What do you think?                            2   I agree.

c   How about ...?                                3   What's your opinion?

d   Good idea.                                    4   I don't know if I agree.

e   I'm not sure about that.                      5   In my opinion, we should ...

f   I'm afraid I strongly disagree               6   I'm sorry, I'm not sure what you
    with that.                                        mean.

g   I'm afraid I don't understand.               7   I suggest that we ...

The management team are discussing plans for the opening of a new shopping mall. Choose the correct phrases in their conversation.

**A**  *So, as you know we're here to discuss the opening of the new mall.* **Some ideas / Any ideas**[1]*?*

**B**  *Yes, I think we should* **invite / to invite**[2] *a famous person to do the opening.*

**C**  *That's* **good idea / a good idea**[3]*. And how about* **to have / having**[4] *a music group play live in the mall?*

**A**  **I'm not sure / I don't sure**[5] *about that. It would be very noisy. I know, why don't we* **giving / give**[6] *away free gifts to the first 100 people to arrive?*

**B**  **I don't think I agree / I think I don't agree**[7]*. Wouldn't it be too expensive?*

**C**  **I'm agree / I agree**[8]*. It would cost too much. Although maybe we could give away some balloons to children.*

**A**  *Good idea. Let's do that. And* **who should we invite / we should invite who**[9] *to open the mall?*

## A company website

**1**  Complete the advertisement using words from the box.

user-friendly   graphic   hosting   video   provide

**VJH** Website Design

We _____ [1] creative services for companies who need top quality website design solutions. We can help your company maximize its potential by making sure that your website is both attractive and _____ [2].

**We offer:**

» logo and _____ [3] design
» _____ [4] and multimedia content
» web- _____ [5].

**VJH** For integrated website design solutions

**2**  Write your ideas for improving your company's website.

Example

I think we should have more pictures on the website.

_____

_____

_____

## Case studies

**1**  Choose the word which doesn't go with the verb.
a  supply          products / discussion / needs
b  expand          managers / business / capacity
c  promote         a product / level off / a company
d  take            over a company / chances / demand
e  improve         profits / losses / performance

**2**  Complete the sentences using words from Exercise 1.
1  They've bought a new factory because they want to _____ _____ .
2  We're going to use a new advertising agency to _____ our _____ .
3  'World of Paper: we _____ all your paper _____!'
4  Increased sales _____ _____ by 11% last year.
5  Did you hear that Bigcity Bank has _____ _____ BV Bank?
6  In these difficult times I don't think we should _____ _____ by expanding the business.

## Business writing: correct the mistakes

The e-mail message below was distributed after a progress meeting at GSI, a computer game developer. There are three mistakes in each of the following:

- spelling
- verb tenses
- punctuation and capital letters
- prepositions

Underline the 12 mistakes and correct them.

---

✉ **E-mail message**

**From:**     Ben Harker
**To:**       Development team
**Subject:**  Todays meeting

It was good to see you all at the meeting, and many thanks to your input today. Here's a brief sumary of the main points:

- We have finish the first version of the Pirate Voyage game. Congratulations to the team!
- We have decided to cancell the Grand Prix Challenge game.
- Last week we have started revising the graphics of the Dark Knight game.

During the next three months, we will completing the Dark Knight project and carry out consumer testing of Pirate Voyage, We will also begin work on a game to replace Grand Prix Challenge at July.

as you know, our next meeting will be on Wendesday, June 15, on 10:00 a.m., and we will brainstorm ideas for a new game.

Please be ready with plenty of ideas and suggestions.

Ben

---

1 _____
2 _____
3 _____
4 _____
5 _____
6 _____
7 _____
8 _____
9 _____
10 _____
11 _____
12 _____

# 12

# Speaking in public

**MODULE 12.1**  How to give a presentation

**1**  Put these parts of a presentation in the correct order. The first one has been done for you.

a  Now, let's look at the product itself … ☐

b  My name's Sang-Hyun and I'm going to be introducing our new kitchen product. ☐

c  I'm going to start by talking about the product specifications, then I'll show you the product, and finally I'd like to talk about the special features. ☐

d  Good afternoon. I'm very pleased to be here and I thank you all for coming. ☐ *1*

e  First of all, the Supermixer is a new concept in mixing machines … ☐

f  Thank you for your attention. Does anyone have any questions? ☐

g  Finally, I'd like to turn to the special features of the product … ☐

h  Well, I think that's all we've got time for at the moment. ☐

**2**  Match the words (1–5) with their definitions (a–e).

1  introduction   a  a good feeling about your ability
2  structure       b  the work you do before a presentation
3  preparation    c  short pieces of writing to help you remember something
4  notes           d  the beginning of a presentation
5  confidence     e  the way a presentation is organized.

## MODULE 12.2 — A short presentation

Use your notes below to write the introduction and ending of your presentation.

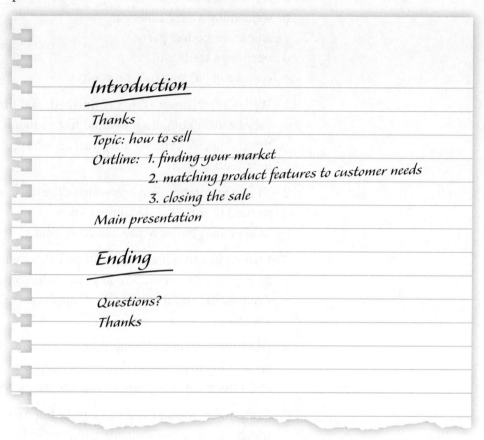

**Introduction**

Thanks
Topic: how to sell
Outline:  1. finding your market
          2. matching product features to customer needs
          3. closing the sale
Main presentation

**Ending**

Questions?
Thanks

## MODULE 12.3 — Thanking and saying goodbye

Put the words in the sentences in the correct order.

a  have / attention / I / your / could

_____?

b  for / evening / I'd / to / you / thank / like / this / coming

_____

c  hope / I / meal / enjoying / you're / I / as / as / the /much / am

_____

d  help / your / stay / my / I'd / to / for / like / during / thank / you

_____

e  with / in / I / forward / you / future / to / working / look / the

_____

f  propose / like / I'd / toast / to / a

_____

**1** Match these extracts from five speeches with the situations below.
  a  launching a new product ☐
  b  welcoming a new colleague ☐
  c  an end-of-course party ☐
  d  opening a trade fair ☐
  e  completing a construction project ☐

1  Well, Center Tower is finally finished, and I think you'll agree that it is a very beautiful building. I would like to thank everyone on the team, from the architects to the security guards, who worked so hard during the past four years.

2  I'd like to congratulate everyone in the development team who worked so hard to meet the deadline. I know some of you have been working 24 hours a day, but now you can relax a little!

3  I would like to welcome you all and also thank everyone who helped to organize this event. We have something for everyone: presentations, discussions, and manufacturers' displays. I'm sure it will be a great success.

4  I'd like to introduce Kenny Foo, who has recently joined us in the accounting department. We're very happy to have you on board, Kenny, and I hope you are going to enjoy working with us.

5  Sadly, today was our last class, but I hope we will all be able to keep in touch. I'm sure you'll all agree that we've learned a lot of English and I'd like to thank Ms. Davis for her excellent teaching.

**2**  Complete the sentences. Use words and phrases from the speeches in Exercise 1.

a  What do we call a group of people who work together?

We often call them a _____.

b  What's a _____?

It's the date or time when a job must be finished.

c  What's an _____?

One meaning is an occasion such as a conference or product fair.

d  What does it mean if you welcome someone on _____?

It means you are happy to have them as a member of your group.

e  What does to _____ mean?

It means to e-mail, phone, meet, or write to someone regularly.

**MODULE 12.5**

## An end-of-course speech

Read the end-of-course speech made by a student. Complete the speech with the words below.

patience    miss    appreciate    thank (x2)    toast    forward    attention

'OK. Could I have your _____¹ for a minute? I'd like to _____² everyone for coming, and for your hard work during the course. Of course I'd especially like to _____³ our teacher Jane. I really_____⁴ her hard work and _____⁵. Looking ahead, I'm sure what we've learnt will be useful. I will _____⁶ our classes, and I look _____⁷ to working with you again sometime. In the meantime, I would like to wish you all the best of luck. So, finally, I'd like to propose a _____⁸. To Jane!'

**1**   Read the e-mail messages and check (✓) the correct answers below.

---

✉ **E-mail message**

**From:**   Toshi Okada
**To:**   Stephanie Gershon
**Subject:**   My trip

Stephanie,

I arrived home yesterday, and I'm still suffering from jet-lag! I really enjoyed my trip to California. It was a great success and I'd like to thank you for all your help. I was pleased to meet the design team and look forward to working with them. I hope to see you again sometime.

Best wishes,

Toshi

---

✉ **E-mail message**

**From:**   Kwang-ho Park
**To:**   Dick Riley
**Subject:**   The dinner party

Dick,

I really enjoyed the dinner party last night. It was great to meet everyone in the Export Department. Thank you very much for organizing everything. I promise to send some photos in the next few days.

See you again when you visit Seoul next month.

Kwang-ho

---

✉ **E-mail message**

**From:**   Paul Beltois
**To:**   Marina Gonzalez
**Subject:**   The goodbye party

Marina,

Thanks so much for the party on Friday. The food was superb and everyone was so kind. Thanks, too, for the palm. It's going to be very useful in my new job. I hope I can figure out how to use it!

Regards,

Paul

---

| | Toshi | Kwang-ho | Paul |
|---|---|---|---|
| a   He might meet the other person again. | ☐ | ☐ | ☐ |
| b   He just received a gift. | ☐ | ☐ | ☐ |
| c   He's going to send some photos. | ☐ | ☐ | ☐ |
| d   He just left the company. | ☐ | ☐ | ☐ |
| e   He just returned to his country. | ☐ | ☐ | ☐ |
| f   He's definitely going to meet the other person again. | ☐ | ☐ | ☐ |

**2**   You recently visited a supplier in the US. Your host, Jill Flood, showed you round the factory and the city. Write a short thank-you e-mail to her.

# Answer key

## 1 Meeting people

### MODULE 1.1

**1**  a 3   b 2   c 1   d 4   e 2   f 1   g 4   h 3
**2**  a 3   b 5   c 1   d 6   e 2   f 8   g 4   h 7

### MODULE 1.2

a  Hello, I don't think we've met.
b  Do you know each other?
c  This is Jim Murray from the Boston office.
d  Have you been waiting long?

### MODULE 1.3

**1**  1 for   2 of   3 from   4 in   5 on
6 with   7 to   8 by

### MODULE 1.4

a  When did IBM start up?
b  What does IBM make?
c  Does Bridgestone supply tires to Ford?
d  How much of Bridgestone's sales come
   from non-tire products?
e  Where is Silas Chou based?
f  Which markets is the Tommy Hilfiger
   Corporation expanding into?

### MODULE 1.5

**1**  a, d, c, b
**2**  c, b, a

### MODULE 1.6

**B** Are you **enjoying the** conference?
**A** Is this your **first trip to** Korea?
**B** Who do **you work** for?
**A** And **you**?
**B** What does your **company** do?

### MODULE 1.7

**1**  Dear Ms Addison,
I'm the Business Development Manager at 'PP Plastics'. You
may remember that we met at the 'Plastics for the Future' fair
recently.
We produce a variety of plastic products for household use.
We have two factories in Australia. We plan to introduce our
products in Western Australia in the near future.
I will be in Perth next week and would like to meet you to
discuss possibilities for working together.
I hope you have time to meet me. Please let me know when
would be good for you.
Best regards,
Sylvia Jones.

**2**  (Example answer)
Dear …
I'm writing following our meeting at the IT fair recently. As
you may remember, my company develops software for the
finance industry. We have an office here in Shanghai with a
team of 40 developers.
I would like to meet you to talk about how we can help you
with your software needs.
I hope you have time to meet me. Please let me know when
would be good for you.
Best regards

**3**  1 a   2 b   3 b   4 c   5 c   6 b   7 a
**4**  a 6   b 1   c 11   d 2   e 7   f 10   g 4   h 12
i 3   j 8   k 5   l 9

## 2 Telephoning

### MODULE 2.1

**A** Hello. Could I speak to Ann Jones, please?
**B** I'm afraid she's away from her desk right
now.
**A** I see. Do you know when she'll be back?
**B** I'm sorry, I don't know.
**A** Could I leave a message?
**B** Of course. May I have your name, please?
**A** Vic Kaplan. That's K-A-P-L-A-N. Could you ask her to
call me today?
**B** I'll give her your message, Mr. Kaplan.
**A** Thank you very much. Goodbye.

### MODULE 2.2

1  Max Pitt speaking
2  What can I do for you?
3  I'm calling about our order.
4  Could I speak to Max Pitt, please?
5  One moment, please
6  I'm afraid he's not in the office right now.
7  Could you put me through to his assistant, please?

### MODULE 2.3

a  This is Mr van Donk. Could you ask Tom to send me the
new catalogue as soon as possible?
b  Mr Chung speaking. Could you tell Tom my new e-mail
address is ddchung@asek.com
c  This is Rosa Velasquez. Could you tell Tom I'll return
the damaged items on Monday?
d  This is Mr Shibata. Could you ask Tom to fax me my
flight details?
e  Mr Neff speaking. Could you ask Tom to meet me at
Harry's Bar at 8:00p.m. this evening?

## MODULE 2.4

a Bobby Deng called. He won't get to the reception until 8:00p.m.
b Meryl Woo from Woo Enterprises called. Please send her the order by fax
c Tony called. Please send him Sharon White's phone number as soon as possible.
d Mike Kibby from the Hotel Plaza called. He needs to talk to you about the conference booking. Please call him back on 234-5788.

## MODULE 2.5

a Could I
b Could I
c Could you/Would you like to
d Could you
e Would you like to/Could I
f Could I
g Could you

## MODULE 2.6

Jill Murray from M-Trade **33** called. Please call her back before **7p.m.** Her number is **993-4768**, extension **258**.

## MODULE 2.7

**1**
| a | Tom Asher | b | Polly Yang |
| c | 11:30 a.m. | d | Mr. Takagi |
| e | Toshiba | f | Yes, he will. |
| g | His visit next week. | h | No, it isn't. |

**2**
| MESSAGE FOR | Sam Cash |
| Taken by | [your name] |
| Time | 3:55 p.m. |
| Date | April 27 |
| MESSAGE FROM | |
| Name | Ms. Spinner |
| Company | MV Music |
| Tel. No. | 912-1985 |

☐ will call back later

☑ please call him /(her)

MESSAGE
It's about the new contract. It's very urgent.

## MODULE 3.1

**2**
2 I'm choosing the photos at the weekend.
3 I'm meeting the printers on Thursday.
4 I'm sending the catalogue copy to the printers by next Thursday.
5 They're sending me the proofs next Tuesday.

## MODULE 3.2

**1**
| 1 today | 2 tomorrow |
| 3 the day after tomorrow | 4 this Friday |
| 5 this weekend | 6 next Thursday |
| 7 a week from next Tuesday | |

## MODULE 3.3

1 I'm going to a conference.
2 I'm working at home.
3 I've got a management meeting in the morning.
4 I've got a sales presentation.

## MODULE 3.4

2 How about the beginning of next week, Monday?
3 Sorry, we're meeting the visitors from head office on Monday morning.
4 OK, Monday afternoon?
5 Sorry, after lunch we're making a presentation. It's a really tight schedule.
6 I see. How about at the end of the week then?
7 Well, the visitors are leaving on Wednesday. How about Thursday at 10 o'clock?
8 Great. See you then.

## MODULE 3.5

**RUBY** *Hello Antonio. It's Ruby speaking.*
**ANTONIO** *Hi Ruby.*
**RUBY** *I'm sorry, but I can't make the meeting on 27th, because I've got to go on a training course.*
**ANTONIO** *OK, I understand.*
**RUBY** *Could we meet on 28th at 11 o'clock instead?*
**ANTONIO** *Sorry, I've got a meeting then. How about 2 o'clock?*
**RUBY** *Yes, that's fine. See you then.*
**ANTONIO** *Looking forward to seeing you. Bye.*
**RUBY** *Thanks. Bye.*

## MODULE 3.6

| 2 a visit | 3 a time | 4 tennis |
| 5 swimming | 6 a meeting | |

**MODULE 3.7**

**1**  a  Adam Ho                     b  the new catalogue
       c  10.00a.m.                    d  She's meeting someone.
       e  at 2.00p.m.                  f  Yes.

**2**  *(Example answers)*
       Date:    27 January 2009, 08:35
       From:    Sue Wang
       To:      John Smith
       Subject:
       John
       Could we meet sometime to discuss the training plan? How
       about tomorrow at 3p.m.?
       Sue

       Date:    27 January 2009, 08.42
       From:    John Smith
       To:      Sue Wang
       Subject:
       Sue
       Sorry, I'm working at home tomorrow.  How about the day
       after, 9 a.m.?
       John

       Date:    27 January 2009, 09.55
       From:    Sue Wang
       To:      John Smith
       Subject:
       John
       9 a.m. on Thursday is fine.  See you then.
       Sue

## 4 Company performance

**MODULE 4.1**

a 4     b 2     c 1     d 3

**MODULE 4.2**

**1**  1  rose sharply              2  fell slightly
       3  remained constant        4  fell sharply
       5  rose slightly

**2**  In April sales rose slightly from $2 million to $2.5 million.
       In May they remained constant. In June they fell slightly to
       just over $2 million. In July they rose sharply to just over
       $3.5 million. In August they fell sharply to just under $2
       million.

**MODULE 4.3**

1  ninety thousand
2  ✓
3  ✓
4  ✓
5  ✓
6  two thousand and seven
7  ✓
8  thirty-nine point five billion
9  two hundred and seventy five
10 ✓
11 four thousand
12 two hundred and fifty

**MODULE 4.4**

**1**  a False   b True   c False   d True   e False   f True

**2**  a  Japan's production was highest in 2006.
       b  The UK produced fewer cars than Japan every year.
       c  The USA's production was lowest in 2004.

**MODULE 4.5**

1 at        2 from      3 to
4 by        5 to        6 to
7 by        8 to        9 to

**MODULE 4.6**

**1**  a  Kay Ashton.
       b  Because she canceled the meeting.
       c  Her car broke down.
       d  Yes, Monday at 10:00 a.m.

**2**  *(Example answer)*
       E-mail message
       To:   Tanya Jacobs
       From:          [your name]
       Subject:       Our meeting
       Dear Tanya,
       I'd like to apologize for canceling our meeting on Friday on
       such short notice. I had to attend an emergency meeting. I
       hope it didn't inconvenience you too much.
       How about meeting this week, say on Thursday at 2:00 p.m.?
       I look forward to hearing from you, and apologies once
       again.
       [your name]

## 5 Products and services

### MODULE 5.1

**1** 1 c, e, g      2 b, d, i      3 a, f, h

### MODULE 5.2

a What can the projector do?
b How big is it?
c Who is it for?
d Where can you use it?
e Does it have any special features?
f How much does it cost? / How much is it?

### MODULE 5.3

1 Hyundai is an automobile company. Headquarters are in Seoul, Korea, and they have more than 137,000 workers. Their main activities are car production and research.

2 Mariott International is a hotel company with more than 3000 hotels and resorts worldwide. Headquarters are in Washington D.C., USA and they have approximately 151,000 employees.

### MODULE 5.4

**1** 1 provide      2 design      3 use
4 help      5 install      6 successful
7 developing

### MODULE 5.5

**1** a Can I get you something?
b Would you like a coffee?
c What are your plans for next year?
d Where will the office be?
e How old are they?
f How many lessons do they want a week?
g How much will it cost?
h Will the lessons be in our office?

**2** c 1    e 2    a 3    g 4    b 5    f 6    h 7    d 8

### MODULE 5.6

**1** GPS

**2** (Example answer)
It's made of metal and maybe plastic. You use it in the kitchen to heat food quickly. It uses electricity. It's smaller than a cooker.

**3** dictionary, toothbrush, laptop, bicycle

### MODULE 5.7

**1** 1 c    2 f    3 j    4 g    5 b
6 h    7 e    8 a    9 d    10 i

**2** b complimentary close     c inside address
d date line     e letterhead
f reference number     g signature block

## 6 Talking about decisions

### MODULE 6.1

**1** 1 Because    2 and    3 as a result
4 Because    5 so    6 As a result
7 and

**2** b they liked her cards very much.
c the cards sold well.
d sales decreased after a few years.
e the new cards were very popular.

### MODULE 6.2

(Example answers)
Sales rose so profits increased sharply.
Profits increased sharply because sales rose.
Demand increased because they carried out an advertising campaign.
They carried out an advertising campaign so demand increased.
Profits rose sharply so employees received a bonus.
Profits rose sharply and as a result employees received a bonus.
Employees received a bonus because profits rose sharply.
They had problems with quality control so demand fell.
Demand fell as a result of problems with quality control.

### MODULE 6.3

**Across**
1 profits     5 agreement     9 expand
12 control     14 fell     15 share
16 consensus

**Down**
2 result     3 involved     4 weekly
6 improve     7 increased     8 campaign
10 bonus     11 attract     13 brand

### MODULE 6.4

**1** protect the environment
attract business customers
launch a product
publish a book
offer a luxury service
improve brand recognition
carry out an advertising campaign

### MODULE 6.5

**1** 1 Shall we buy
2 I don't think so.
3 How about buying?
4 people don't need
5 interested in
6 of buying
7 successful

## MODULE 6.6

**1**  a  August 3.
   b  $2,468.75
   c  Yes, he has.
   d  By the end of the month.

**2**  *(Example answer)*
   Dear Mr. Corney,
   I am writing to inform you that we have not received your payment of $5,468.50 for invoice no. N2860 which, according to our records, I e-mailed to you on September 26. I hope that you received the invoice.
   For your convenience, I have enclosed another copy with this letter. I look forward to receiving the payment from you by December 5. If there are any problems, please do not hesitate to contact me.
   Sincerely,
   [your signature]
   [your name]
   [your position in the company]
   Enc.

## 7 Complaints and problems

### MODULE 7.1

1 S    2 C    3 S    4 S    5 C    6 S

### MODULE 7.2

**A** *Good morning, Conex Customer Service.*
**B** *Good morning. This is Mesut Akman from Alpha Engineering.*
**A** *How can I help you, Mr. Akman?*
**B** *I'm afraid I have a complaint about the new photocopier you installed yesterday.*
**A** *I'm sorry to hear that. What's the problem?*
**B** *The paper jams.*
**A** *The paper jams?*
**B** *Yes. When we make double-sided copies, it jams every time.*
**A** *I see. I'm very sorry about the inconvenience. I'll send someone round right away.*
**B** *I'd appreciate that. Thank you. Goodbye.*
**A** *Goodbye.*

**2**  1  complaint        2  damaged        3  problem
   4  inconvenience    5  care           6  unfortunately
   7  wrong            8  appreciate

### MODULE 7.3

**1**  1  043762        2  Sept. 28        3  golf bags
   4  DB306          5  35              6  25

**2**  **A** Good afternoon, Sportworld Wholesales. How can I help you?
   **B** Good afternoon, This is [your name] from Uno Sports here. I'm afraid there's a problem with our last order.
   **A** I'm sorry to hear that. Could you give me the order number?
   **B** Yes, it's 044812.
   **A** One moment, please. Yes, according to our records, you placed the order on October 4. You ordered 300 baseballs, model number BX303.
   **B** I'm afraid that's not quite correct. We ordered model number BX403, not BX303.
   **A** I'm sorry about that. I'll look into it right away.
   **B** Thank you.

## MODULE 7.4

**1**
| | | |
|---|---|---|
| 1 f, i | 2 c, l | 3 a, j |
| 4 e, h | 5 b, k | 6 d, g |

**2** *(Example answers)*

1 **A** Excuse me, there's a mistake on my bill.
  **B** I'm sorry, sir / madam. I'll change it right away.

2 **A** I bought this TV set here yesterday but it isn't working.
  **B** I'm sorry about that. I'll get you a replacement.

## MODULE 7.5

**1** There isn't any coffee / hot water.
There aren't any towels.
The Internet / lamp isn't working.
The room is noisy / cold.
The mini-bar is empty.

**2**
1 A There aren't any pillows.
  B I'll send some to your room right away.
2 A The air con isn't working.
  B I'll send someone right away.

## MODULE 7.6

**1**
| | | |
|---|---|---|
| 1 possible | 2 clearly | 3 suggest |
| 4 apologize | 5 polite | |

**3**
a Order number E276.
b This morning.
c They sent the wrong amount.
d A copy of the order form.
e Send ten more cameras as soon as possible.

**4** *(Example answer)*

To        George O'Hara
Date      [today's date]
From      [your name]
Subject   Order number BN56

Dear Mr. O'Hara,

I am writing with reference to the delivery of computer monitors, order number BN56, which we received yesterday. Unfortunately, you sent us the wrong model. We ordered the PS25 monitor but we received the PS20. I am attaching a copy of the order form for your reference.

I would be grateful if you would send us the correct model as soon as possible.

I hope that future orders will be checked carefully before dispatch.

Sincerely,

[your signature]

## 8 Checking progress

### MODULE 8.1

**A** *How are you doing with my travel arrangements for the trip to India?*
**B** *Fine. I've reserved all your flights.*
**A** *Thanks. And what about hotels?*
**B** *Yeah. I've made reservations at the Taj in Mumbai and the Intercontinental in Delhi.*
**A** *Sounds good. And the meeting with Mr Mehra?*
**B** *I haven't arranged an appointment with him yet. He's busy at the moment, but I'm going to speak to him soon.*
**A** *OK. And what about the dinner on the first night?*
**B** *Don't worry. I've booked a table for four at the Taj.*
**A** *That's great. One more thing – should I take a gift for Mr Mehra?*
**B** *I know. I've already bought something nice for him.*
**A** *Perfect. Thanks for your help.*

### MODULE 8.2

**1**
| | | |
|---|---|---|
| 1 How's | 2 How are | 3 Have you |
| 4 How's | 5 Have you | 6 Have you |

**2** a 4  b 6  c 1  d 3  e 2  f 5

### MODULE 8.3

*(Example answer)*

Dear Kim

I'm pleased the trip is going well. I've already finished preparing the presentation and I've booked your flight tickets for the conference. I haven't booked the hotel or taxi yet, but I'll do that tomorrow.

See you soon.

[your name]

### MODULE 8.4

**2**
a True
b False. He worked as a product development engineer previously. He is now the CEO of Owl Power.
c False. Four years.
d True
e True

### MODULE 8.5

**1**
1 False. They are going to install equipment in April.
2 True.
3 False. They are recruiting staff now.
4 False. They started advertising in January.

### MODULE 8.6

| | |
|---|---|
| 1 checked | 2 Did you have |
| 3 wasn't | 4 Have you heard |
| 5 was | 6 arrived |
| 7 I called | 8 seen |
| 9 haven't | 10 phoned |
| 11 leave | 12 said |

### MODULE 8.7

**3**
| | |
|---|---|
| a Far Eastern | b taxi |
| c two | d 13:00 / 1:00 p.m. |
| e three hours | f 19:30 / 7:30 p.m. |
| g Mr. Li | |

## 9 Future prospects

### MODULE 9.2

**1**
1. I think people will want electric cars.
2. Do you think people will read newspapers?
3. Most people will work at home.
4. I don't think people will smoke.
5. I don't think there will be any demand for fixed line telephones.

### MODULE 9.3

*(Example answers)*
2. I'll **help** you.
3. Good. Maybe I'll **watch** it.
4. OK. I'll **phone** the teacher.
5. Almost. I'll **send** it to you soon.
6. Then I'll **go** by bus.

### MODULE 9.4

**1**
| | | |
|---|---|---|
| 2 may | 3 certain | 4 convinced |
| 5 probably | 6 might | 7 sure |
| 8 likely | | |

**2**
a. certain / convinced / sure
b. certain / likely
c. definitely / probably
d. may / might
e. definitely / probably

### MODULE 9.6

**1**
a. Sunshine Stores:
   a chain *of* supermarkets
   known for good products *at* a reasonable price
   are spending a lot *on* expansion – buying supermarkets internationally
b. Lux Autos:
   specialize *in* making luxury cars
   good reputation *for* quality
   cost *of* skilled workers is high
   are investing a lot *in* research (cars of the future)

### MODULE 9.7

**2**   a False   b True   c True   d False   e False

**3**   *(Example answer)*
Dear Ms. Henderson,
It was a pleasure to meet you last week. As you requested, I am sending you next year's catalogue.
I would like to draw your attention to our new lipsticks on page 3. We think that the Serena line, with its wide range of brand new colors, will be a top seller next year.
If you have any questions or would like to inspect any of our products, please do not hesitate to contact me.
Sincerely,
[your signature]
[your name]
[your position in the company]

## 10 Regulations and advice

### MODULE 10.1

**2**
| | | |
|---|---|---|
| a True | b False | c True |
| d True | e False | f True |
| g False | h False | |

### MODULE 10.2

**2**
| | | |
|---|---|---|
| a can | b can't | c don't have to |
| d can | e have to | f don't have to |
| g have to | | |

### MODULE 10.4

1. It's a good idea not to drink alcohol during the flight.
2. Good advice.
3. It's best not to eat a lot during the flight.
4. It's best to wear comfortable shoes.
5. Good advice.
6. You should get to the airport in plenty of time.
7. Try to adjust to the new time zone as soon as possible.
8. I wouldn't eat a lot of fatty foods before the flight.

### MODULE 10.5

**2**
b. Do you think I should arrive on time?
   Oh, yes. It's a good idea to arrive no more than ten minutes late.

c. Do you think I should leave on time?
   Oh, yes. It's a good idea to leave at 7 p.m. if the party ends at 7 p.m.

d. Do you think I should drink only a little alcohol?
   Oh, yes. It's a good idea to drink no more than one beer or mixed drink per hour.

e. Do you think I should talk to people?
   Oh, yes. It's a good idea to go up to people you don't know and introduce yourself.

f. Do you think I should apologize if I accept and don't attend?
   Oh, yes. It's a good idea to contact the host the next day.

### MODULE 10.6

*(Example answer)*
Dear Shane,
I'm happy to give you some advice about your visit.
Firstly, it gets very cold here in winter, so you should definitely bring warm clothes. You should also bring formal clothes for the office. Office culture is quite formal and you should always try to be on time for meetings.
If you're invited to someone's home it's usual to take fruit as a gift. Also, you should remember to take off your shoes when you enter someone's home.
Looking forward to seeing you soon.
[Your name]

## 11 Meetings and discussions

### MODULE 11.1

a 3    b 5    c 6    d 2    e 1    f 7    g 8    h 4

### MODULE 11.2

**1**  1 think          2 about          3 idea
       4 suggestions    5 should         6 agree

**2**  a 4    b 3, 6    c 4    d 1, 2, 5

**3**  a 5    b 3    c 7    d 2    e 4    f 1    g 6

### MODULE 11.3

1 Any ideas?
2 invite
3 a good idea
4 having
5 I'm not sure
6 give
7 I don't think I agree
8 I agree
9 Who should we invite?

### MODULE 11.4

**1**  1 provide        2 user-friendly    3 graphic
       4 video          5 hosting

### MODULE 11.5

**1**  a discussion    b managers      c level off
       d demand        e losses

**2**  1 expand capacity
       2 promote, product
       3 supply, needs
       4 improved profits
       5 taken over
       6 take chances

### MODULE 11.6

1 Today's (punctuation)
2 many thanks for your input (prepositions)
3 summary (spelling)
4 We have finished (tenses)
5 cancel (spelling)
6 Last week we started (tenses)
7 we will complete (tenses)
8 Pirate Voyage. We will (punctuation)
9 in July (prepositions)
10 As you know (punctuation)
11 Wednesday (spelling)
12 at 10:00 a.m. (prepositions)

## 12 Speaking in public

### MODULE 12.1

**1**  a 5    b 2    c 3    d 1    e 4    f 8    g 6    h 7

**2**  1 d    2 e    3 b    4 c    5 a

### MODULE 12.2

*(Example answer)*
Introduction
Good morning and thanks for coming. My name's (your name) and I'm going to be talking about how to sell. I'm going to start by talking about how to find your market, then I'll talk about matching product features to customer needs, and finally I'll talk about closing the sale.
Ending
That brings me to the end of my presentation. Does anyone have any questions? I'd like to thank you for your attention.

### MODULE 12.3

a Could I have your attention?
b I'd like to thank you for coming this evening.
c I hope you're enjoying the meal as much as I am.
d I'd like to thank you for your help during my stay.
e I look forward to working with you in the future.
f I'd like to propose a toast.

### MODULE 12.4

**1**  a 2    b 4    c 5    d 3    e 1

**2**  a team          b deadline       c event
       d board         e keep in touch

### MODULE 12.5

1 attention      2 thank        3 thank
4 appreciate     5 patience     6 miss
7 forward        8 toast

### MODULE 12.6

**1**  a Toshi    b Paul     c Kwang-ho
       d Paul     e Toshi    f Kwang-ho

**2**  *(Example answer)*
Dear Jill
I'm writing to thank you for showing me around your factory and around San Francisco during my visit. It was great to meet everyone at the factory and to see some of your beautiful city. I really enjoyed our seafood dinner too! I hope to visit again one day.
I look forward to working with you.
Best wishes
[your name]

**ANSWER KEY**